TURNAROUND UK

TURNAROUND UK

Trusting and empowering
UK citizens to create growth

Robert Tyler

worthpublishing.com

First published 2025 by Worth Publishing Ltd
worthpublishing.com

Printed and bound in Great Britain by CPI Group (UK) Ltd, Croydon CR0 4YY

British Library Cataloguing in Publication Data
A catalogue record for this book is available from the British Library

ISBN 9781903269442

Cover and text design by Anna Dadswell

To Gladys Dorothy Tyler

Contents

Acknowledgements   ix

Author's note   x

Introduction   Setting the scene   1

PART ONE   **Urgent action needed**   21

Chapter 1   Growth and productivity   23

Chapter 2   Taxation changes   41

Chapter 3   Health and social care   51

Chapter 4   The law and access to it   61

Chapter 5   Defence   67

Chapter 6   Housing and land use   73

Chapter 7   Energy supply   79

Chapter 8   Education and inclusion   85

Chapter 9   Immigration and emigration   93

Chapter 10   Transport in the UK   99

Chapter 11 Climate change and the environment   103

Chapter 12 Governing standards, fairness and censorship   107

Chapter 13 A balance sheet to date   119

PART TWO Broad changes for the future   123

Chapter 14 Voting and democracy   125

Chapter 15 Long term debt and the emotions behind it   131

Chapter 16 Relationships with other countries: a world view   137

Chapter 17 Developing community feeling   141

Conclusion   146

Acknowledgements

I am profoundly grateful to the team at Worth Publishing and my editor, Andrea Perry, who gamely unravelled confusion, insisted on crystal clarity, spotted repetition and stimulated further review, and that was not just on the early drafts! Inevitably throughout my experiences in life I have also been helped by many wise men and women, and some astute children too numerous to mention, who have enabled me to develop the views and actions I propose. I hope I have listened carefully, understood and learnt well.

Nor could I have written this book without the support of Lucy Wilton, together with tolerance and encouragement from my wife Diana. Thank you all.

Author's note

In researching and writing this book, I have needed to draw on statistics from a variety of sources and look at the evidence base of the evidence base. In a number of cases, it has been difficult to obtain definitive figures because of subsequent adjustments, a variety of definitions of the same terminology (for example gross GDP, real GDP, nominal GDP or GDP in US dollars) to aid international comparison or simply because some figures are not available or accessible to ordinary citizens. There will also be different dates reflecting the time period over which the book was written (the early months of 2025), and what was available then. Overall, the general argument and conclusions of the book are not affected by this, in my opinion.

To empower would-be entrepreneurs of any age going for growth, there are some tips on my website, robertbtyler.com

TURNAROUND UK

Introduction
and setting the scene

Hello! This is a book written by an ordinary citizen for ordinary citizens. If you still believe that anything is possible and still have even a slight belief in the virtue of democracy and the power of the people to effect change for good, this is a book for you. I want to take you on a short journey through the policies of today's government and show how you can help it refocus on things that really matter to us all.

I'm going to look at every major aspect of current government policy and recommend changes which I believe put the needs of our citizens first and provide hope for a brighter future to which we can all contribute. Whilst we are alive, the UK belongs to its citizens: and, as citizens, we belong to the UK and can help make a better future for all our children. Give us hope, and we will follow! Inevitably that means looking at both top level strategic decision making, because that affects everybody, but also trying to ensure in detail that the poorest and most disadvantaged people in the UK are first in line to benefit from those changes.

I want a government mindset which instinctively believes in helping to distribute fairly the income it receives from all of us. I hope that having read this book, you'll agree with and embrace the spirit of this priority: even if you disagree with some of what I set out, or the ways I believe would enable this to happen.

I'm writing in the early part of 2025. I was born in London and after school and college, my first job was a clerk in the

Housing Application department of a London Borough Council. I then joined a large manufacturing company based in London and worked my way up to director level, before private equity helped me start my own business. I sold that business and have since devoted my time trying to help disadvantaged young people find opportunity to succeed in life. My parents were not wealthy, and I know what hardship feels like.

Even though you may not agree with every decision or policy I recommend, I am asking you to think deeply about the policy decisions I propose in the belief that we would all benefit from them, and then, take matters into your own hands and vote for a change in our democratic voting system. A change that would mean all our views will be truly represented in Parliament so that there is hope for a better future for everyone, our families and the people we care about, and society at large.

So, let me give you my conclusions first. In the first instance, I want our electoral voting system to be changed to Proportional Representation (PR) so that the mix of opinions in Parliament matches the strength of support for them in the country. I believe this would galvanise more of us to feel involved and included, and that the time is right to do this: polls* show that the public want this too.

Secondly, I believe the present overriding Government strategy of pursuing growth is correct. But I believe that the *execution* of that strategy so far is deeply flawed, as a result of those in power not being clear what growth actually means and entails for UK citizens, and also what growth is for. I also believe that for any Government strategy to succeed it must gain the trust of its voting citizens first and operate thereafter by consensus, not diktat. These are difficult demands, and I have attempted to show how I believe they can be

* Do Britons support shifting to proportional representation? | YouGov

achieved. I also conclude that a growth strategy has to have a clear purpose, and that purpose has to be to benefit all citizens with the people genuinely most in need at the head of the queue.

I will refer only to ideas for important actions and policies involving the UK central government departments, which I'm calling UK Central Government, or UKCG. Devolved governments in Northern Ireland, Scotland and Wales differ slightly on a number of subjects but, as far as I am aware, what I suggest could have universal application. The ideas I put forward would not be irrelevant to the devolved powers, since the crucial aspects of most policies are retained by UKCG.* I have assumed that UK Local Authorities or Councils, and devolved city Mayors, do not deviate from UKCG policy! In the financial year 2024/25, UKCG spent £82.6 billion** in devolved government grants, but did not specify how that should be spent.

This book is clearly about politics, so I'll declare my political approach. I am a liberalist in principle: that means I believe that the power of government should be limited by law and that government should create a constitution and/or provide institutions which protect the rights of its citizens (for a good description of broadly what that entails see *Liberalism and its Discontents*, Fukayama 2022). I am a pragmatic voter (meaning I could vote for any party whose policies and values came closest to my thinking, if I were dissatisfied with them all).

I have no specific expertise, but a variety of experience. I have invented some things still in use today, though it's not relevant here

---

* The reserved powers of the UKCG in relation to
  Scotland can be found at Devolved and Reserved Powers | Scottish
  Parliament Website, to Wales at senedd.wales/how-we-work/our-role/
  powers/ and to Northern Ireland at education.niassembly.gov.uk/
  post-16/work-assembly/making-legislation/pow

** wheredoesitallgo.org

to say what they are. I have a lot of ideas, some radical, based on what I've experienced, and others I consider to be common sense or logical. I'm not writing this in order to set up a new political party! But simply to contribute concrete suggestions to the debate around the many areas where UK badly needs improvement. I'd be delighted if some of the proposals were supported and taken up by those in a position to put them into practice. Or, why be modest? If they all were. But it's also fine with me if you disagree: as I've mentioned, the object for me is to encourage the belief that politics can lead to the betterment of all our lives, and we all have something to contribute.

In order to make what follows understandable, I also have to declare, I think, a number of other basic assumptions I've made about people and growth. These assumptions also underpin my approach to Turnaround UK, and are as follows:

I HUMAN ASSUMPTIONS

- Each person on planet Earth is different
- Each person shares a desire to have a good life on their terms
- Each person has feelings and wants to do things
- What people eventually do is more important than what people say they will do
- The context of where and when someone is born is important
- Ultimately consensus amongst the UK population about actions affecting them is crucial to creating lasting change

2 GROWTH ASSUMPTIONS

Throughout this book I have taken the object as being to recommend ways to improve the lives of us all. I believe the way to do this is to pursue growth for the country, providing the benefits of that growth are fairly shared amongst the whole population.

- Gross Domestic Product (GDP) for the UK, an amalgam of all the goods and services sold by UK in a year to a final user, is the measure of growth used. The figures for this are not perfect but are the best available guide. Growth can both be described in absolute terms for the country as a whole, or in terms of output per person: both are relevant in this book.

- To me, growth means personal wellbeing as well as economic satisfaction, which may well include achieving these as part of a better life for our families and the people significant to us. As the measure of growth is money for UKCG I have used the way that money is created as a measure for each citizen. Growth has always been about added value from human effort, achieved manually or intellectually. Nevertheless, the world's population has to live within the confines of the world's natural resources and its weather and position in the universe. Clearly, we cannot mine for oil or transfer farming land to housing forever, as both oil and farming land are finite resources. Those factors are a constraint on some growth ideas.

- Further, at the moment all advanced countries have to borrow from each other to survive each year, since all governments are spending more than they receive from households (primarily) and from other sources. This cannot go on forever either. At present the reason there are still lenders to indebted countries is ultimately that the lender knows that the citizens in the countries doing the borrowing own far more assets than the governments themselves, and that governments will always try to tax those assets before bankruptcy. Climate change has thrown a spanner into those working assumptions, because increasingly, citizens' assets, particularly property, are being destroyed by fire, floods, drought and high winds as a result of the rapidly changing climate.

I shall thus make the point in Part 2 of this book that climate change is the single most important factor governing growth, and that finding alternative, more efficient or more productive ways of using resources, including how to deploy us as human beings, is the only way to add value to our lives.

WHAT TO DO WITH THE FRUITS OF GROWTH

The question of how UKCG handles growth is just as important as how it creates it.

The benefits of growth can be handled in three fundamental ways. Either UKCG can redistribute wealth amongst the population, pay off debt, or a combination of the two. In this book I suggest the latter choice. I'm advocating for a greater engagement of the UK population with the ways and means of creating growth, and I also want UKCG in turn to respond to citizens' needs more effectively and more promptly than hitherto. On debt, I'll highlight the need to tax the better off and the dangers of that source of tax being compromised by excessive borrowing and a failure to tackle climate change. I am also concerned that the fruits of growth are not squandered on unproductive UKCG expenditure.

These human assumptions and the key questions to address may seem obvious enough, yet they determine which policies are likely to succeed. Accepting the above assumptions also makes obtaining human consensus challenging! It also explains why some MPs understandably resign from a party with a huge majority in Parliament, because it's unlikely that any two people would absolutely agree in detail on anything that might or should happen when a new policy is formed for legislation. So you'll see as we go that I welcome multiple differences of opinion: I view them as both healthy and understandable since no two people are the same (with the possible exception of identical twins). *Vive la différence* as our French neighbours might say, even after Brexit. That's also the reason I believe changing our voting system to one of proportional representation (PR) (Chapter 14) rather than the current 'first-past-the-post' system is key to growth. Only then can a common objective of more fairly distributing the fruits of a growth strategy be properly fulfilled.

The barometer for testing whether the fruits of growth are being properly distributed is to some extent evidenced by the number of citizens below the poverty line. At present the poverty line in the UK is an ever-changing number, since it is calculated as being 60% of average income after housing costs. Housing costs are rent, mortgage payments, building insurance and water rates. The last published levels were in November 2024, according to Trust for London.* For example, the outer London poverty level was £373 per week for a single person household. That's roughly equivalent to the minimum wage of £12.21 per hour for a 35 hour working week after tax. The level for a couple household was £643 per week. There is also a destitution line defined by the Joseph Rowntree Foundation as households missing any two of the following 'essentials for living', which are having a home, food, heating, lighting, shoes and basic toiletries. In 2023 the Foundation reported that one million children in the UK were destitute. I would want the fruits of growth to wipe out child destitution first, and I believe my policies would at least do that.

Wealth and inequality

But there is, I think, alongside a desire to eradicate child destitution an equally profound issue in today's UK, which is the question of

* London's Poverty Profile | Trust for London

inequality in wealth, and thereby of opportunity for UK citizens.

The focus on material wealth in the last 60 years has exacerbated tensions between those who have and those who do not. In the UK, this tension has been epitomised by the right versus left debate in politics, which itself is the product of our voting system. In 2010 an excellent book written by two distinguished researchers, entitled *The Spirit Level* (Wilkinson & Pickett, Penguin) stated that equality is better for everyone. Their conclusion: *"What we need is a society that recognises the benefits of greater equality",* and I agree with this. They also state, and research has shown* that citizens in more equal societies enjoy better physical and mental health than those in less equal societies..

This may well be a laudable intention but, as is common in political discussion, it's far easier to state the problem than to find a solution. In this book I'm attempting to offer practical solutions which I hope would support UK citizens to remember we can have a common cause: that being cooperative is better that being confrontational: that friends yet to be made are also out there in the community at large as well as those we've known for a long time: that a team can achieve more than an individual: and above all else, *to judge others by their actions rather than what they say they will do.* I believe that UK citizens and UKCG reaching out to one another in this way would ultimately help to level the playing field of opportunity.

The most likely stimulus for a more equal society is climate change, which is already affecting not just UK citizens but the citizens of the whole world, both rich and poor. The increasing cost of action needed to save everyone on our planet, rich and poor, will have to be paid by the rich. The rich, with their vast resources, have the most assets to lose, and the most to contribute as the only major

* blogs.worldbank.org/en/opendata/inside-the-world-bank-s-new-inequality-indicator--the-number-of-source of tax for world governments to turn to. This might seem an odd view today but after 2050 looks well-nigh unavoidable.

So, it's vital that UKCG clearly identifies what it intends to do with the fruits of growth. Money is the means of exchange and therefore the means of change - which is why we need higher value from what we do from our GDP numbers both as a nation and as individuals. Consequently, when I say there is a need for urgency, I am also saying that urgency is highly relevant to the objective outlined above: the greater sharing of the wealth created. UKCG has the power to change citizens' perception of what is worthwhile through describing the ultimate objective of their policies, and having the good sense to desist from blame, humiliation and discord in public pronouncements.

After reading this book, readers may still accuse me of being either too right wing or too left wing because of the policies I propose. My answer is that in order to fly, you need both a right and a left wing! And flying together is what UKCG and UK citizens need to do when it comes to growth and using the fruits of growth well.

WHAT SOURCES OF GROWTH ARE THERE?

I have said growth is measured by GDP. GDP is the value of goods and services bought by the final user and generated by UK from four sources in a given time frame (such as financial year 2024/25). The sources of value are:

- Household expenditure
- Government expenditure
- Investments, both private and government
- Exports (after deducting imports)

There is a significant difference between the UK and the 27 members of the European Union (EU) when you look at the percentage of

GDP represented by household expenditure. In 2023 in the UK, that percentage was 61% and in the EU, 52% on average (the average for France and Germany was 54%). In China it was 39% and, in the USA, 68%. This tells us something about the economies of other countries, and where growth has to come from.

In the USA, which has the advanced world's highest percentage growth factor from households, the growth would need to come from exports. Surprisingly perhaps, the USA currently imports more than it exports, and the net effect on their GDP (October 2024) was minus 4%. This might have a bearing on President Trump's interest in imposing tariffs on imported goods. In the UK, we currently have the same problem, where the net effect of exports on GDP is minus 2.5%. In China, exports exceed imports, and government expenditure as a proportion of GDP is much higher than Western government averages. This means China needs to encourage domestic expenditure to maintain growth. I will argue in detail that growth comes from people, not from Governments, in Chapter 1.

Household Expenditure as % of GDP - 2023

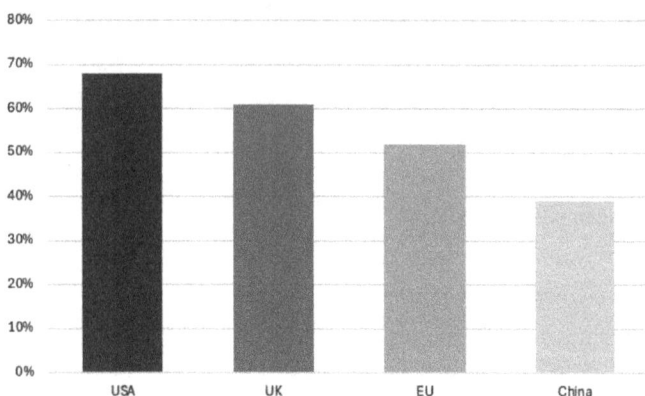

Source: World Bank

THE INFLUENCE OF TAXATION POLICY ON GROWTH

All governments rely on the wealthiest individuals for tax or loans to exist at all. Broadly, the more autocratic the government, the smaller the number of wealthy individuals amongst the total population, and that even applies to a 'pretend' democracy where the available candidate choice is controlled by those already in power such as Russia.* History has shown that power corrupts, and absolute power corrupts absolutely. UKCG has to face the problem that it needs to tax the wealthiest individuals in order to be able to run the government and support the less wealthy. But if it removes too many avenues for individuals to become wealthy, the government will fail everyone, including the less wealthy, and thus extend inequality between citizens, as the poorest have nowhere to go.

Two examples of this issue of UKCG domestic tax policy over-taxing the rich UK might be firstly, where the present government (January 2025) decided to impose VAT on private schools. This is in line with any government's policies which will always be to tax the rich the most. However, the current government did not decide to apply VAT to private health bills. The result is that in isolation, the policy on private schools is seen as illogical and therefore viewed as a tax on better-off children's opportunity; and thus vindictive, by those able to afford it. The closure of private schools is also bad for growth. Secondly, the decision to penalise many of the highest taxpayers, the so called non-domiciled millionaires and formerly welcomed investors in the UK, could risk victimising and antagonising too many high taxpayers at the same time. This would clearly be bad for growth and tax revenue for quite some time.

Applying VAT to private health bills, although a logical and

* statista.com/statistics/262687/countries-with-the-highest-rate-of-millionaires/

understandable move, would risk antagonising too many high taxpayers at the same time against the government, unless the economy was booming. This would be bad for growth, as I believe it's reasonable to assume that those that can afford private education and health are largely among the top 10% of income tax payers; according to The TaxPayers' Alliance* in the tax year 2024/25, 10% of income tax payers paid 60% of income tax receipts. Almost certainly, that top 10% of income tax payers will be influencing our growth prospects.

All forms of heavy taxation on the rich are available, but there is a tipping point which could destroy the current government, from which there would be a very long road back. The rich are an engine of growth as spenders and investors, and therefore an overzealous UKCG wanting to drain their resources could backfire, with much lower tax receipts if too many of the rich emigrate.

At the time of completing this book, the USA had decided to apply extra taxation to imported goods from across the world. The effect of this is to heighten inequality amongst citizens of all the nations affected. In the largely free trade world where previously such tariff taxes were rare, many products bought by USA citizens came from relatively poor countries in the Far East and Africa, thus by and large improving the lives of those countries' citizens. Imposing tariffs on those countries whose populations cannot hope to reciprocate by buying USA products will suffer hugely for no good reason. Imposing tariffs in general has increased the cost of living for USA citizens who will demand increased wages to compensate. If tariffs are not reversed, the current USA administration will eventually be ousted. Another example of the dangers of overreaching Government interfering with the freedom of citizens to grow.

* Briefing: share of income tax paid by percentile: The TaxPayers' Alliance

To return to our example in relation to tax policy: if private schooling and private healthcare are viewed as more efficient by the citizens who can afford and prefer them, then that is a good reason for not taxing them with VAT but rather trying to learn from the aspects of better performance which have driven choice in the private sector, for the benefit of the public sector. UKCG could also learn from what works in other advanced countries.

HAS UK GROWTH BEEN RE-DISTRIBUTED FAIRLY THIS CENTURY?

How much better off financially are UK citizens in this century, as a result of UKCG growth? The Bank of England inflation calculator, which uses the Consumer Price Index (CPI) to compare that in December 2000 with December 2024, says inflation has been 85% in this period. UK GDP in the same period increased by 100%. In the same period, the average full time employment gross pay has increased by 99%. So, UK citizens' pay has reflected the growth in GDP in the century thus far. UKCG dictates citizens' hourly pay, having created the minimum wage; this has increased by 281% in the same period. Despite this, pay growth still parallels GDP growth, which suggests that the minimum wage has not helped beneficiaries as much as intended, since gross pay has moved up at a much slower pace. Overall, citizens have shared the benefits of growth in gross pay with Government growth in the period, but it is highly doubtful if those benefits have improved citizens' lives equally, when the numbers of destitute children remains far too high, as I described earlier.

As far as UK citizens are concerned, I have tried, wherever possible, to propose policies which favour the younger generation and particularly the disadvantaged. Our children, grandchildren and great grandchildren need the freedom of thinking and ability to act to withstand and nullify the bad effects of climate change. They also need to be able to do that from the comfort of a secure home.

UKCG MANDATE FROM UK CITIZENS

In the UK 2024 election only 59.7% of adults voted. Excluding 2001, this was the lowest election turnout since 1918. About one third of voters voted Labour, so the mandate was roughly 20% of people entitled to vote (9.7 million out of 48.2 million entitled voters), meaning that 80% of voters either had or might have had a different opinion. My conclusion is that people remain dissatisfied with the direction and competence of successive governments because they cannot see 'growth', in its widest sense of personal and financial improvement, for them, their families and society at large from the actions of any particular government. In constituencies where there has always been a substantial majority for Labour, Liberal or the Conservatives, many voters don't bother to vote because they think their vote will be wasted. In fact I also believe that our voting system is designed to encourage people *not* to vote, rather than to vote, and I will address this fundamental issue in Part 2, since it's the foundation of future citizen involvement in making decisions which affect us all.

As a result of this poor mandate of 20% of voters, I will look at many aspects of UKCG policy through my 'growth' lens to see if they correlate with the human assumptions and citizens' objectives I have outlined: hence growth is the first subject I tackle. It also happens to be one of the few areas of policy UKCG cannot control. It can only *invite* growth, by creating the right atmosphere for it. UKCG has created the right atmosphere over centuries, by both design and accident. As my assumptions underline, and voting history confirms, growth comes from people wanting, feeling and being able to go for it!

Turnaround UK looks at each aspect of UKCG government control and management in each area of policy, as well as some areas which government seeks to control but has no obvious mandate to do so (such as, in my view, censorship). In each chapter on a UKCG policy area, I first ask two key questions:

> **1   Should the UKCG 'control' this particular policy making area?**
> In this book, the word *control* means creating a policy in law or having the legal right to pursue a policy, and the right to control the total cost budget of that policy and its satisfactory outcome.
>
> **2   Should the UKCG 'manage' the policy created?**
> In this book, *manage* means there must be a necessity for UKCG to manage the operation of the policy itself.

The difference between control and management, which I set out above, is a crucial distinction and doubtless the subject of much argument.

In part, I have made this distinction to define who to applaud or criticise for carrying out the current policies for running the country. It's also an attempt to be fair to UKCG, which, whilst it has a public duty to *respond* to the fundamental need of the UK population to be safe, housed, healthy and cared for when necessary, cannot be expected to meet those needs centrally: except where it is crucial that it must do so (such as in the case of defence). The areas which UKCG *must* control and manage are *tax* (Chapter 2), *defence* (Chapter 5), *immigration* (Chapter 9), *climate change and the environment* (Chapter 11) and *governing standards* (Chapter 12). In areas addressed in other chapters, UKCG management is either not possible or not essential, in my view.

This book contains a number of radical proposals in the Chapters in Part 1 on *health* (Chapter 3), *housing* (Chapter 6), and *education* (Chapter 8), and in Part 2 on *community living* (Chapter 17).

These proposals are not just ideas. I've researched each one in consultation with many people who would be affected positively by the changes. In some cases I've prepared software and/or legal paperwork to show how these proposals would work in practice, and, where appropriate, have ascertained that related funding would be available. In one case, one of the money saving ideas - the housing rent guarantor scheme - has already been accepted by UKCG, but surprisingly has not as yet been activated or fully explored.

This book is in two parts.

PART I URGENT ACTION NEEDED TO TURNAROUND THE UK

Chapters 1-11 look at every aspect of Government control and asks the questions above: should UKCG control this aspect, and should it manage it? The answers to these questions are followed by my recommendations for immediate policy change within the next 12 months.

My recommendations do not cover every aspect of each policy area: the ones I've included are designed to produce growth by creating the right atmosphere for growth, as above, and should be viewed in that light. Chapter 12 is about standards and fairness which apply to all governments and describes current issues which I believe need resolving by UKCG: otherwise citizens will not trust UKCG and will ultimately vote it out of power and lose yet more confidence in democracy.

Chapter 13 summarises the financial impact of the income and expenditure policies in my short term solutions to the UKCG 'problems', listed in Chapters 1 to 12.

PART 2 BROADER ISSUES FOR THE FUTURE

Reviewing and considering the whole of Part 1, Part 2 describes what I would wish to see later, after reflecting on the challenges and success of implementing the proposals in Part 1. It focuses on four things: *voting and democracy* (Chapter 14), *long term debt and the emotions behind it* (Chapter 15), *relationships with other countries* (Chapter 16) and *developing community feeling* (Chapter 17).

All the numbers I use are from the latest published material I could find, which I reference. I've tried to avoid errors of fact but there may be some, since I'm human, and these are my responsibility. The most important change of all, galvanizing overall public understanding and support, will likely take longer than twelve months!

I've tried to make the ideas straightforward, to make them accessible to as wide an audience as possible. Inevitably, to do so invites the critic to say, *'Life is not as simple as that'*, which is obviously true, but if there were sufficient popular belief in this approach to growth then I'd be more than satisfied. Human desires and reactions are usually straightforward. Endless semantic debate exacerbates progress when there are only 100 years of life available to most of us to make life better for everyone!

Wherever possible, I have tried to cost financial decisions which affect taxation and human endeavour, using the latest published data. Some of my recommendations will not have a costed base either because I haven't found one to draw on or they are too subjective to assess.

Inevitably there will also be areas of policy which I haven't covered, which essentially means that I've not thought that they are an essential ingredient to the purposes of this book at the moment. I've accepted those items in the October 2024 Budget not affected by my proposed changes as adequate, at least for the first twelve months. Benjamin Franklin said nothing is more certain in life than death and taxes, and I would add - the inevitability of change.

The overall purpose of this book is to encourage people not to give up on politics; to think about some of the issues I discuss, which affect all our future lives, in a positive way. It's critical for us as ordinary citizens to be and to feel part of decision-making both locally and nationally, and to believe in and trust our governmental institutions to fairly guard our interests: but at present that belief and trust is chronically low. I hope that the views of a fellow citizen will inspire others to feel similarly able to think up and get behind solutions to the issues we all face, and that collectively a better way forward can be found for all. We may not be born equal. but we have an equal right to be able to live as well and as long as we can and to support one another to do likewise.

In this book, my whole approach to us as citizens, particularly children, is based on the Belonging Model®, to which I am a contributor. This model was written with respect to what support a child needs to feel they belong and can thrive. Whilst clearly the relationship between UKCG and citizens is not parental, it is - or should be - one of having the duty to create the circumstances under which we can all feel secure, able to thrive, and maybe even feel loved, or at least, truly valued. And that's what I would call, at its heart, liberalism.

THE BELONGING MODEL®

DEVELOPING
MUTUAL TRUST

RESPECTING
& MANAGING
EACH OTHERS'
FEELINGS

PROMOTING
A CHILD'S
SELF-AWARENESS
& SELF-ESTEEM

ENABLING
A CHILD TO FEEL
SECURE, LOVED &
ABLE TO THRIVE

© Worth Publishing Ltd

PART 1

Urgent action needed

CHAPTER I

Growth and productivity

Control	Should UKG control this?	**NO**
Manage	Should UKG manage this?	**NO**

Everybody wants to be better off than at present. That's one of the key drivers of human energy. Irritatingly for UKCG, however, there is no foolproof way for government to control or manage growth since it is a human creation based on individual willingness to cooperate. What UKCG can do however is to create the right atmosphere for growth, and hope for the best: so I will offer some ideas as to how it can do that.

THE PROBLEM - HOW TO ACHIEVE LASTING GROWTH

Growth cannot be legislated for, since it is a matter of behaviour. When we look at Gross Domestic Product (GDP) per person, there is a big difference between the US and UK. According to the World Bank, GDP in 2023 was $82,769 per person in the US, and $49,463 in the UK.*

There are advantages in the US around internal market size and being the owner of the world's most traded currency, but the biggest difference for the UKCG is the US population's attitude to growth,

* GDP per capita (current US$) | Data

commonly referred to as the American Dream. The fact that many entrepreneurs from a wide variety of backgrounds in the USA have made huge sums of money helps provide role models for the dreams of the mass population as well (it can also, sadly, instil despair in the minds of those who do not succeed, when the 'dream' becomes a nightmare).

One of the many cultural factors which may contribute to growth may be connected with the number of days leave from work in the USA compared to the UK. In the UK there is a statutory requirement for all employees to receive four weeks annual leave, plus bank and religious holidays. In the USA the law varies from State to State but there is no legal requirement for a standard annual leave for employees. Although the issue of leave in the USA is changing, as it is in the UK with the development of working from home and pressure for a four-day week, the starting base for leave from work is still much less generous in the USA than in the UK.

As I explained in the Introduction to this book, both the USA and UKCG rely on consumer confidence which propels household expenditure to sustain GDP (61% UK, 68% USA). Other advanced countries relying less on household expenditure at home within their GDP output will be those relying more on exporting to, more than importing from, other countries, particularly to the world's biggest consumers, USA and China. That's likely why President Trump is choosing to impose tariffs on imports, since at present, the USA imports in value more than it exports. In the UK on the other hand, currently (December 2024) imports also exceed exports by about 2.5% of GDP, and we are struggling to increase exports after Brexit and especially now in the face of potential US tariffs. To increase GDP in the UK, that only leaves increasing UKCG expenditure or household expenditure

In theory, the only way to get growth from home consumers is to reduce their taxes to give them greater spending power. However, at present UKCG is doing the opposite by increasing taxes on consumer income by not increasing tax bands by inflation, and restraining future pay by increasing the employer's national insurance contributions to UKCG.

That leaves increasing government expenditure as a growth engine. UKCG is already concerned about its level of debt. Increasing expenditure before generating increased income from growth is a risky undertaking, as it's likely to have the impact of unnerving lenders to UKCG. I've also noticed a trend (*see below*) that households reduce their debt in line with UKCG increasing its debt. The graph shows that over the last sixteen years, UKCG debt as a percent of GDP increased from 36% in 2008 to 95% in 2024, whereas household debt as a percentage of disposable income declined from 155% in 2008 to 120% in 2024. Citizens share the worry about debt as much as UKCG.

Debt as a Percentage of Disposable Income

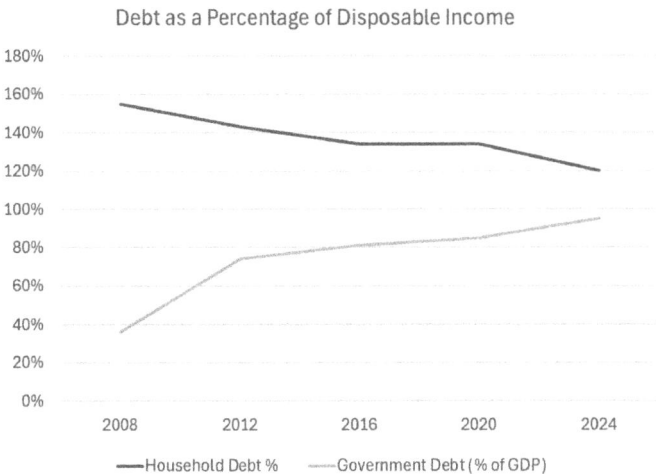

UNDERSTANDING PRODUCTIVITY

Thus if UKCG has a growth policy, and it would be strange if it did not, then its attitude to what happens and the policies it chooses should be perceived to be supporting growth. UKCG investment does not control growth: people do. People need to be initially financially encouraged to go for growth through the tax changes I outline in the next chapter, and I believe they would subsequently be encouraged when they see the benefits of growth in terms of improvement of services and their environment, and better wealth redistribution across the country.

As currently defined, UK growth occurs when UKCG produces more value (sale or GDP) added per head of population than before. That statistical measurement is affected by inflation, net immigration and the relationship of £sterling to other currencies: so it is not a perfect measure.

But it is a simple truth that if you can do the same thing more quickly (efficiency) and charge more for it (inflation) you are better off personally. That is clearly true if you are the only source of income for your household and you charge by the hour to get that income. For UKCG, the main source of income is the citizen, so citizens need to respond in this manner for the UK to achieve growth.

Most people think the biggest driver of productivity is money in the form of capital investment, but I question this, based on past experience of projects such as HS2 and the third runway proposal at Heathrow, and my own experience in business. I believe the driver of productivity is the individual. The individual must both feel it is the right thing to do, be willing to do it, repeat doing it and enjoy that process. Also, being more productive involves working harder and smarter, which requires good management in a form which Government openly supports, and where there is skilled and humane commercial control, by which I mean the relationship between the working individual, the management and the purpose of the task is respected, fully understood and supported.

The UK economy is now primarily based on services, largely people providing information, support and guidance to other people. Obtaining productivity in that type of business cannot be based on investing in better machinery, as it was in product manufacturing.

HOW TO IMPROVE PRODUCTIVITY

So there are two key principles to improving productivity in services. Firstly, the task must be clearly defined and assessed by the person required to do it as to whether all of it needs to be done, or whether it can be done more simply, by cutting out unnecessary checking, for example. Secondly, through assessment of how the task is best performed, and, in particular, focusing on establishing a good relationship with the setter and the beneficiary of the task. In hospitality for example, when entering a hotel or restaurant, the warmth and focus of the staff on the task of looking after you will likely determine or at least influence how much you spend. That warmth is not an expense for the supplier, but it is productive.

Another example might be if a government employee was responsible for assessing an application form for supply of a frequently used service and pointed out that 20% of the questions were irrelevant to a decision being made, thus saving time for the supplier and the government employee. I suggest these key elements are the reasons why growth and productivity rely on people and their relationship to the task and customer.

CAPITAL EXPENDITURE AND PRODUCTIVITY

Of course, money invested is important. But witnessing what happened to the UKCG's massive investment in the HS2 rail project shows that money thrown at productivity without the personal commitment of all those involved is wasted. The disputes between the land owners who were compensated for lost property, the contractors and the government, as well as the complaints from residents in affected areas, and finally the unwillingness of UKCG to fund connecting HS2 to Euston station, actually meant a loss on the colossal investment, since the project hasn't delivered the productivity from time saving which was the rationale for starting it.

A similar major investment proposition is presenting itself now to UKCG concerning the use of AI (Artificial Intelligence), where UKCG is looking at big investment without the personal commitment of those affected. A cost vs benefit analysis for AI is tempting to ignore when a trawl of internet information appears to provide unlimited time saving and therefore cost saving for UKCG, and thus likely to increase productivity per hour or per person. Yet AI also adversely affects people, and therefore productivity, and has the potential to have a net negative effect.

Why is this? The first answer is the AI abuse of current intellectual property (IP) status. Millions of individuals make their living from IP - songwriters, authors, software developers, artists, publishers, musicians and inventors for example - and millions of businesses rely on brand protection, copyright protection of information on the internet, including that accessed by subscription, and registered trademarks. AI could constitute an attack on the creative industries which are a unique strength of the UK economy if applied without consultation with and consideration of rights holders.

The second potential AI negative is to question what job upheaval costs are involved and what the newly unemployed would do for a living. Where should AI be used for growth first? The answer is likely to be in the UKCG area of interest where there is a lot of real data which, used better, could produce greater efficiency, where present productivity is very poor and where there is a need for a lot more staff. This might apply to the NHS,* but creates even greater pressure if the impact on patients and staff is not adequately considered. For example, if AI improved time spent on diagnosis and paperwork for GPs to allow them to make more home visits to patients, would they actually do so?

Who knows the right questions to ask AI? In response to *"How should I tidy up my office?"* AI might well remove the occupant as well as extraneous paperwork if not clearly instructed! And how much might it cost UKCG to defend against malign use? Good reasons to proceed with care on investment direction and cost, and important for UKCG decision makers to carry the support of the citizens of the UK.

GROWTH AND CONFLICTING PRIORITIES

The current growth objective also presents conflicting priorities, the most important of which is the conflict between using fossil fuels in response to and their adverse impact on climate change. Oil and gas, linked to electricity, have been the driving force for growth in the last 100 years. Pragmatism means we have to hang on to their coattails as we phase in alternatives for power generation: though we know that doing so continues to drive climate change. The extent to which this is so also depends on the productivity of those engaged in quickly finding the renewable energy alternatives to fossil fuels (*covered in* Chapter 11).

Finally, the UK has both an ageing population, requiring longer life health care, and an older workforce less able to carry out the heavy lifting and other manual tasks involved in housebuilding and product distribution which are essential for a vibrant economy, as well as there being the need for greater investment in relation to meeting the challenge of climate change than in earlier times. These pressures

* england.nhs.uk/long-read/artificial-intelligence-ai-and-machine-learning/#summary

are exacerbated by the fall-out from the Covid epidemic which sadly has left perhaps two million adults on long term sick pay and unable to work. The pressure on the remaining population will demand that the benefits of productivity improvement must be felt by all, and may well necessitate importing foreign labour.

The cost of responding to these demands is adding to our long term debt mountain quite quickly at present. Getting UKCG income to equal UKCG expenditure going forward is not just desirable, it is essential if UKCG wants to meet its fiscal rules and not risk high borrowing costs. The importance and detail of both these issues is covered in Part 2, Chapter 15.

SOLUTIONS
ACHIEVING GROWTH AND HIGHER PRODUCTIVITY
In summary, these are the measures I propose: the details of the taxation changes follow in Chapter 2.

I   Encourage entrepreneurs
Encourage existing and emerging entrepreneurs with the changes to corporation tax, income tax and stamp duty outlined in the next chapter on taxation.

2   Create the right atmosphere for growth
a)   Growth requires a sense of urgency
This involves UKCG doing quite a lot of things which have already been budgeted for more quickly, such as compensation for the Post Office personnel and the Infected Bloods scandal victims. UKCG doing things too slowly is a bad advert for growth - *"They are all talk and no action"*. Paying all due a substantial equal sum across the board within budget, and settling further need individual cases later, would demonstrate commitment.

b)   Delay consideration of the Employment Rights Bill until its impact on growth is fully assessed

There needs to be balance in the Bill between the justifiable need to protect employees from unfair treatment and the need for any business to survive competitively in the world of commerce.

Relations between workers' unions and bosses or shareholders have fundamentally changed from the 20th to 21st Century.   The management class did not exist until about 1920, so workers had previously been clearly at the behest of the wealthy owner bosses and needed to get together to obtain better working conditions. This continued through the period 1920-2000 (roughly), where workers needed unions to improve their position because of poor management and indifferent shareholders.   Today the vast majority of us are workers and employees. Shareholders are now largely directors in small to medium sized businesses, and the shareholders in public and larger companies are usually individuals within investing institutions whose role is to pressure the management for better results.

Delay would provide the opportunity to make amendments in line with c) below and allow a broader review of the potential disruption to growth impact of such wide-ranging changes in the workplace at the moment.

c)   Modify the current Employments Rights Bill to balance the need for business growth with safeguards for employees

Firstly, we all rely on the properly organised and affordable supply of the essentials for living. That requires employee cooperation and consensus, irrespective of UKCG diktat. There is no doubt that there are still bad managers and indifferent shareholders which engender employee strikes, walk outs and genuine grievances that need resolving. Yet, I believe there is a greater sense in business and in government that we are all in this together than before.

There are certainly good intentions behind the Bill, particularly on avoiding harassment of all kinds at work, something big companies, such as McDonalds or Amazon, have had to defend, but some law firms and charities as well. Good companies and institutions know that keeping all employees content and loyal is the key to growth. Badly run private sector businesses will not last for long in today's competitive market.

But as it stands, the Bill is a serious disincentive for owners of new businesses to take on people at the outset, and will also alarm existing small business owners who are already under cash pressure to perform in what is currently an extremely challenging marketplace.

Those parts of the Employment Rights Bill which put entrepreneurs off from starting a business (the right to demand a union representative, sick pay and challenge unfair dismissal from day one: the right to work from home: the banning of all zero hours contracts even if preferred by the employee: restrictions on the fire and rehire rules which could prevent many companies from going under when they get into financial difficulties) should be either extracted from the Bill or modified to protect both the employee *and* the employer.

Secondly, businesses and the people who run them are likely to be pragmatic and that means being sensitive to social movements or concerns such as EDI (Equality Diversity and Inclusion). As all businesses ultimately have final user customers, that sensitivity makes good sense as well as being socially responsive. Most companies will be genuine in that belief. Some companies may simply say so but ignore it in practice. In the USA where there has been a marked change in political philosophy with Donald Trump, US companies may well toe the political line pragmatically in public and disdain EDI principles, but that should not affect UK owned companies here.

In the UK there is a lot of evidence that the needs of all stakeholders, the importance of good governance and environmental awareness are now key considerations for management policy. The issues of climate change, sustainability, pollution and waste are reflected in shareholders' demands on management, as water companies know well.

For an example of my point, a good number of companies are now volunteering to give staff private health care as a reaction to the problems of obtaining prompt diagnosis and treatment in the NHS. This is an example of employers responding to the outside world reality affecting their business. It makes sense to both, since staff earn more, sooner, following illness, and work longer (if they feel supported and are healthier), which creates better productivity: and the business benefits accordingly. It would be surprising if this had come about as a result of a union initiative, but it reflects the current *'We are all in this together'* management approach of the best firms.

In the top 50 of the 100 Best Places to Work in the UK list this year* were huge US enterprises such as JP Morgan, Mastercard and Microsoft, as well as a wide range of other companies and support services reflecting a common management style and approach, rather than a political background.

UKCG is repeatedly saying it is relying on UK businesses to grow. Only people can make this happen. It is far better to have everyone onside in that endeavour, with a modified Bill which would seek a better balance of representing the interests of the work force, existing and potential, and business owners. Thus a suitably modified Bill would be good for companies doing the right thing, good for employees and good for growth.

* Best Places to Work UK 2025 | Glassdoor

*d)   Strengthen the power of the CMA, the Competition and
      Markets Authority*

The purpose of this lesser-known UKCG organisation is to protect consumers from monopoly control of key parts of the market for goods and information. Astute large companies are very good at using their dominant position to constantly raise prices and freeze out competition. A government authority which supports young businesses to enter markets dominated by a few is extremely good for growth in the UK. UK entrepreneurs also have a fine record of creating new companies, particularly in the computer-based tech area. Competition can be the driver of growth and excellence. The CMA should also work with the Europeans who have a similar concern about monopolistic control. UKCG should strongly resist the entreaties of big companies seeking overreaching powers. Such resistance would send a positive signal to business leaders of the future.

3   Require Local Authority accounts to be audited and improve supplier access

In order to improve productivity within Local Authorities (LAs) two changes need to be effected, the auditing of annual LA accounts which will expose areas of activity requiring greater efficiency, and offering wider access to contracts from small to medium sized businesses.

a)   Audit accounts

In order to improve UKCG productivity it first needs to know what money is wisely spent now. In 2024, according to The TaxPayers' Alliance (TPA taxpayersalliance.com) more than 90% of Local Authorities (LA) had not published audited accounts in the last four accounting years. This means that taxpayers have no idea whether their money is spent wisely and competently or indeed if there is corruption or favouritism of supply. Audit will expose most of this, exert a more disciplined approach to spending and form the basis of future productivity-based savings. Each LA will have differing spending pressures according to its demographics. Accurate accounting will promote accurate and relevant UKCG grants to LAs. With a current UKCG budget for Local Authorities of around £125 billion there is likely to be considerable potential saving from better financial control.

b) *Improve small company access to Local Authority contracts*
At present Local Authorities (LAs) are supposed to treat all suppliers equally. This is a requirement of the Public Contract Regulations Act 2015 Section 2. However, this is often ignored by LAs and currently not always possible. This is because most LAs use a number of different computerised procurement systems such as Oracle or Proactis. The terms and conditions of using that software favour big suppliers for two reasons:

(i) Firstly, the procurement systems vary in detail across the 153 English LAs and need a full time supplier staff member just to understand them but secondly, and more importantly,

(ii) the Terms and Conditions of using the LAs procurement systems require small companies to take big risks. For example, one of the procurement systems used by some LAs require an unlimited guarantee from suppliers against computer hacking, whereas their own guarantee for this is a fixed modest sum. Most directors of small companies would think twice before taking such an unlimited risk, whereas big suppliers would be capable of affording legal defence. There should be a simpler universal LA procurement system for individual orders of £50,000 or less and

no unlimited liabilities for small or personally run
LA business suppliers. For larger LA contracts there
should be no unlimited supplier liabilities unless that
risk is matched by the procuring authority.

4 UKCG must improve productivity of its central staff

In June 2016, 384,00 people worked in the civil service, including
part timers: today the number is 542,000. The increase was due to
Brexit in 2017-2019 and then the Covid outbreak (civilservice.org).
Reverting back to 2016 staff levels would represent an annual saving
before redundancy costs of £7 billion (the average annual cost of one full
time equivalent civil servant is listed as £45,000 on civilservice.org).

Huge reductions and inflows have been a feature of the civil service
in the last 25 years. 100,000 people (cost £4.5 billion) were added for
Brexit negotiations and preparation but that has now finished. Nobody
likes to lose their job, which is why I propose help to retrain (*below*).

If you work through all the policy areas covered in this book,
you'll find some areas where I believe whole UKCG departments
could reduce in size and scope - which would be the basis of public
sector productivity improvement.

5 Local government personnel need to improve their productivity

According to the Economic Observatory in 2022 our public
sector productivity was 20% worse than France and Germany and
considerably worse than the USA. There is a one-word answer to
effect improvement and that is urgency!

As previously explained, it's possible to measure public service in
productivity terms, and one of the key ways to improve productivity
is to reach out to the public, which relies on public service. It has
become normal for people within local government to work part time,

often leaving no-one to carry on with a need requested by the LA, a supplier or citizen, and for departments to avoid direct phone contact by using answerphone and reversion to email contact only. All of this is hugely unproductive for suppliers and citizens as well as the LA. It is of course not only local authorities which have become impersonal: so have many organisations in the private sector, for example banks. Banks retreating from dealing with customers face to face in branches may be why in November 2024, 25% of customers of all the major high street banks were dissatisfied with their customer service (according to statista.com). Nevertheless, the LA's fundamental purpose is to serve the needs of its community.

Virtually everything local government gets involved in is important and often a service response is urgent. The lack of accounting audit mentioned before exacerbates this problem. It is not a question of working longer hours: it is a question of recognising the public need a response quickly. Public service is a fine career and hugely and genuinely appreciated by the public when done well. Service efficiency should be the yardstick of performance, and merit in that efficiency rewarded and recognised appropriately.

One way of raising the level of productivity is to give far greater importance and kudos to the whole concept of public service. UKCG should publish a Local Authority (LA) servicing achievement of the month and make it a national competition award. In other words, encourage good service news and appreciation of the value and quality of public service.

6   Work retraining costs should be tax deductible

The skills required for work are changing rapidly. Figures produced by the World Bank Group for 2022 show UK manufacturing representing 8% of GDP, whereas it was 28% in 1979. The rest of GDP now is largely made up of services, of which the greatest part is computer related and information supply. The essential difference is that work now focuses on mental skills rather than manual ones. People will need to be retrained when savings in staff levels through redundancy are made by UKCG.

Retraining costs of up to £4,000 for former UKCG employees should be deducted as an expense from earnings before incurring income tax for up to four years after the date of redundancy. £4,000 is selected as that would cover most or a significant part of retraining costs, but it is the principle of UKCG helping people to retrain that counts. Retrainers would need to be accredited by UKCG from a list of approved training providers and business apprenticeship schemes, and this could be handled by the huge Work & Pensions Department, since part of their remit is to support the unemployed to find work.

7 Create two-way communication with those who know or might know answers

Currently it is impossible for an ordinary citizen, who may have something helpful to say to UKCG, to actually say it in such a way as to be acknowledged as heard, or to contribute. A citizen can only offer advice or complaint to an MP if they reside in the constituency of the MP. Equally, UKCG does not know who to call on when it needs advice. Local Authorities are equally effectively hidden behind mobile and office answerphones and incoming external emails are often binned at source. How, for example, does the Education Department get to know about initiatives which might help Heads of Schools in problem areas?

At present UKCG relies on well-known advocates to advise on a policy change, or on personal friends and contacts, and rules out the public. Many of these 'experts' form Quangos or are special advisers (spads), and some build a new consultancy business as a result - good for growth, but only for an élite few. This can be a crucial error.

The NHS used to have a commissioning section which invited the public to explore new techniques and procedures and funded invited suppliers with innovative ideas to trial their new health products: but this was summarily cancelled three years ago.

Frequently UKCG resorts to academics who have written on a particular subject. This is fine, but there will be people who have practical experience of the effects of or lack of, or an abuse of, a policy, who are not consulted before a change is made. When a simple Google search often reveals what is already available in most fields, and being provided by whom, UKCG spending £millions asking consultants to find out is wasteful. For example, the previous Government awarded a £19million contract to a business consultancy to investigate how to reduce the number and cost of Educational Health and Care Plans (EHCP) without consulting educational psychologists or providers of mental health tracking services who may have known the answer.

So UKCG could provide the Citizens' Advice Bureaux with (CAB) details of who to contact in each UKCG department, and response times should be within 20 working days. I am choosing CAB as a natural place to visit for information and advice on issues citizens feel strongly about. The advice might just be a leaflet with government contact suggestions, such as you might find in a Tourist Information Office about local places to stay and visit.

8   Change UKCG employee work pensions from defined benefit to defined contribution

Unlike the private sector, where regulation requires pension funds to be capable of meeting their long-term contractual pensioner financial needs, UKCG pensions are simply paid out each year from tax revenue and borrowings. The cost for UKCG this year will be at least £124 billion. The state scheme also has a triple lock device which allows it to accept inflation levels from wage growth or price inflation or 2.5%, whichever is highest. This potential open cheque for UKCG employees and pensioners should cease, and 2.5% annual increase remain. UKCG should also abandon the concept of defined benefit as it cannot afford it. In the process of moving to a defined contribution scheme, some consideration should be given to a part of a pension fund being designed to help faster growing UK companies within the overall portfolio of funding. Pension funds as a whole should be able to generate at least 2.5% annual increase and thus save UKCG the expense and benefit pensioners. The new Dutch pension defined contribution scheme (2023)* involving a fixed benefit element should also be explored by UKCG for its employees.

9   Create an umbrella 'pride of place' organisation: RefreshingUK

UKCG could encourage individuals and communities to volunteer to improve untidy and unsightly areas under a Local Authority controlled plan - a 'pride of place' concept, to improve and enrich the quality of the environment and make it look better. This could be small garden schemes in unsightly areas, litter collection, painting railings/fences, simple repair work, installing artwork, even pothole filling. RefreshingUK could be an umbrella organisation embracing and empowering the many existing charities and volunteering organisations** through providing active support so that UKCG, under the Department of the Environment, could demonstrate its care of and commitment to the environment in which we all live.

* apg.nl
** cleanupuk.org.uk/
   earthday.org/7-steps-to-hosting-a-successful-cleanup/
   localtrust.org.uk/big-local/learning-clusters/love-your-environment/
   groundwork.org.uk/making-your-community-project-more-
      environmentally-friendly/
   peopleshealthtrust.org.uk/funding/health-justice-fund/nature-for-health
   sustrans.org.uk/our-blog/get-active/13-things-you-can-do-with-your-
      community-to-improve-your-street/

CHAPTER 2

Taxation changes

Control	Should UKG control this?	**YES**
Manage	Should UKG manage this?	**YES**

UKCG needs a reliable source of income in order to protect us as a nation. It has to manage this itself, otherwise the state will not be protected.

THE CURRENT PROBLEM

The estimated total accumulated UKCG borrowings or debt at March 2025 are about £2.5 trillion. UKCG's total annual output or sales to the final user (usually called Gross Domestic Product GDP) for the year ended March 2025 is estimated at about £2.6 trillion, just greater than the total outstanding debt.

UKCG receipts for year ending April 5th 2024, were £1,099 billion, about 43% of GDP. In the same year UKCG expenditure was £1,223 billion. That in theory means the deficit of £124 billion has to be borrowed from other people or institutions. As interest rates on UKCG borrowing are currently at least 4% of £2.5 trillion it follows that debt interest will be about 10% of annual UK expenditure. Figures for 2024/25 were not available at the time of writing, but are not expected to show an improvement in the cost of interest on debt.

Put it all this way. If you earned net £40,000 wages/salary a year and you already owed £40,000 and each month you worked you had to borrow £330 to live, you would be worried, and in trouble. That's the UKCG position right now.

Of the £1,099 billion receipts, the breakdown was as follows:

Tax on employment: **41.7% of total receipts**
£277 billion was raised from income tax, £180 billion from National Insurance.

Tax on Consumption: **19.7% of total receipts**
£170 billion from VAT, £25 billion on fuel duty, £21 billion on tobacco and alcohol.

Business taxes: **11.2% of total receipts**
Corporation tax was the fourth largest tax, raising £97 billion: business rates raised £27 billion and £3 billion through the energy profits levy.

Other taxes: **27.4% of total receipts**
There were many small tax contributors of which the major ones were £39 billion of Capital taxes (Stamp duty, Inheritance tax and Capital Gains Tax) and £45 billion of Council Tax. The rest would be other receipts from interest, a range of minor taxes and other payments to UKCG.

As is often said, there are three ways for UKCG to reduce borrowing.

> **Increase prices (primarily tax receipts)**

or...

> **Reduce costs (UKCG expenditure)**

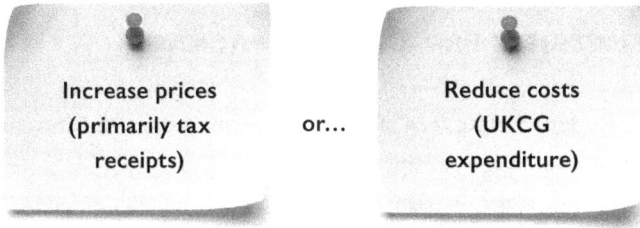

Neither of these are good news for UK citizens. So the third option is the best solution, which is...

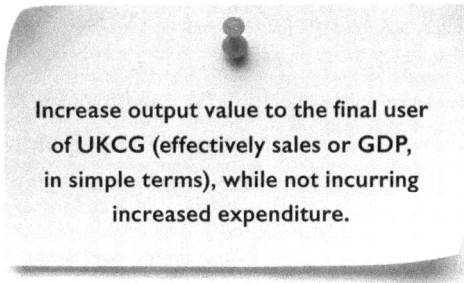

> **Increase output value to the final user of UKCG (effectively sales or GDP, in simple terms), while not incurring increased expenditure.**

This increase in output value is normally called growth and/or productivity. Understanding how we do this is essential, and I will outline a lot of things I believe need to happen to achieve it. In the personal example above, you would need to change job or take on more work to earn net £44,000 a year to stop borrowing each month, and even more if you wanted to pay off your borrowing.

In my solution, I have included provisions which benefit the younger UK citizens on whose future growth relies. I have also tried to be evolutionary, not revolutionary, to try to travel a middle ground based on the here and now. The total effect of all the tax and expenditure changes are compared to the Budget changes in October 2024 in Chapter 13.

SHORT TERM SOLUTIONS:
AN ENTIRELY PRO-GROWTH PACKAGE

1   Reduce employers' national insurance contribution
Estimated tax receipt loss   £21 billion
(based on not reverting fully to the previous 13.8% rate and 2024 numbers above)

Reduce employers' national insurance contribution from 15% to 14% and retain the starting threshold at £9,100 annual earnings.

2   Increase standard VAT from 20% to 22%
Estimated tax receipt gain   £17 billion
(based on the 2023/24 VAT receipts of £170 billion)

Increasing tax on jobs does nothing for growth and in fact retards it, as it upsets all the people who are going to supply growth. Increasing VAT is a tax on consumption which is inflationary, but so is taxing jobs by increasing the costs of suppliers products for consumers.

The reduced rates of VAT - zero (0%) and 5% - tend to help poorer people because they spend proportionally more on food and health products: so reduced rates should remain. VAT in Europe as a whole averages 21.6%, with a variation of 19% - 25%.

3   Decrease corporation tax
Estimated tax revenue loss about £9 billion

Decrease corporation tax for larger companies from 25% to 22.5% with effect from April 2025 and retain for five years. The smaller company rate of 19% should remain for the same period.

Despite this tax loss, there will be compensation in the increased attraction of building and investing in UK companies: the initial tax receipt reduction should diminish and receipts increase over a five year period. In April 2025, the new US administration was threatening worldwide tariffs on USA imports which, if enacted, will have an adverse effect on UK exports to the USA. So this lower tax measure would help UK companies until such time as, hopefully, the USA will realise this measure will lead to substantial price inflation for USA consumers and it will then be phased down or out.

This revised tax rate compares with the world average rate of 23.51% for the year 2023/24 according to the Tax Foundation, whilst the minimum corporate tax rate for large companies was agreed by most countries at 15% in 2024 (the effective rate in Ireland at present). There has been a general trend to reduce corporate taxation over the last 45 years (the world average corporate tax level was 40.18% in 1980). This, and the world increase in borrowings, has been a major driver in the increased standard of living worldwide if measured by income per person.* Thus the effect of this move on UKCG corporation tax income (£97 billion in 2023/24) is likely to be neutral as these corporate tax reductions should be a major driver of growth: and therefore trading profits (the source of the tax take) should grow significantly over a five period.

4   Abolish stamp duty on share transfers
Estimated tax revenue loss - about £3 billion
Any tax benefit is difficult to estimate. However, since trading is currently in decline, signalling that trading in shares, particularly British shares, will be beneficial would be of interest and helpful to would-be UK investors. It would put the London Stock Exchange in line with other worldwide exchanges which do not charge duty on share transfers.

---

* ourworlddata.org

5   Simplify income tax bands

*Estimated tax receipt loss - £1.4 billion**

We should reverse the loss of the tax-free personal allowance for annual income over £100,000 and start the 45% tax band at £100,000 instead of £125,140 (as it is now) allowing the personal tax-free allowance to be reinstated for everyone.

At present, the income tax bands defy common sense. The tax rate begins at 20%, then 40%, then 60%, and then 45%. At present a Headteacher's salary, for example, is around £96,000 per annum. A salary increase of 5% would take that teacher into paying 60% on £800 of that increase and on subsequent increases up to £125,000 as things stand. In addition, that teacher might lose any child benefit allowance. Thus, the reason for the changes I recommend is to ensure that key people in Government and commerce are not presented with a tax barrier to pay, which should serve to attract and, importantly, retain, the best talent.

6   New tax benefit for newly formed British companies

Introduce a new tax benefit scheme for newly formed limited liability companies with exclusively UK home-based directors, which grants freedom from Corporation tax for the first three profitable years of trading, providing those years are consecutive.

There is no cost to this measure because the companies do not currently exist: however this will send a very positive message to entrepreneurs who are the source of high growth rates. Small and medium sized companies already employ 16 million people in the UK, and it may encourage others to take the risk themselves.

---

* The number of people earning over £100,000 is not available, as far I am aware, so the cost is based on a percentile.

7   Increase personal care allowance for care workers by 40%
Estimate tax receipt loss £1.2 billion
based on 1.2 million care full time job equivalence in UK at present

We have a special problem in social care at present, with the biggest factor being the lack of available staff. There is also a great deal of care provided by families in their private homes rather than in care homes.

So I propose that certified and registered care workers be given an increase in their income tax free allowance of 40% bringing it to £17,600 per annum (from £12,570). The 40% bracket should continue commencing at £50,271 as now.

This major initiative would likely be positively viewed by the public which values social care. It is relatively cheap to implement for workers who are generally at the lower end of the wage scale but on whose considerable caring skills we all directly or indirectly rely. It will also have cost benefits related to the NHS too detailed and subjective to estimate. The potential backlash of unions wishing to apply the same allowance to other groups of workers would have to be resisted on the grounds that social care is a special case and has had no other unique increase in return, as far as I am aware.

8   Change property stamp duty on sale
Estimated tax receipt loss - nil

Transfer the stamp duty tax on property purchase to stamp duty tax on sale value of the property using the same percentage rates as apply now (previously paid stamp duty on purchase to be deducted from sale value during the changeover). Stamp duty on purchase adds further cost and pressure on the capacity to afford a property, for the young in particular and also their parents who increasingly try to help fund their mature children in and from their home, where they can. There would be tax income benefit to UKCG forthwith and over time. This would reverse the recent decline in UKCG tax receipts of £11.61 billion in 2023/4 from £15.36 billion in 2022/3. It would also add more freehold owners to the tax base.

9 Reverse the inheritance tax change policies

Reverse the inheritance tax change policies on business relief and that on farmers, both of which clearly act as disincentives for hard working people for whom growth is their business!

10 Prevent non-dom exodus - for now

Reconsider UKCG's relationship with non-domiciled investors (non-doms), all of whom will be in the UK to stimulate growth, and reverse the proposed changes to that regime on 6th April 2025. At the time of writing (January 2025) there are some signs that this might happen because of the departure of over 10,000 big non-dom taxpayers in 2024.

The OBR (Office of Budget Responsibility) also forecast a further 7000 will leave the UK in 2025/26 tax year. The Finance Act 2025 proposes to tax non-doms on their worldwide income and removes virtually all their exiting tax benefits from April 2025. Any review should prevent this mass exodus of non-doms from the UK at least until other tax receipts can compensate.

11 Greatly increase information sharing with the public

The public are entitled to know and understand the thinking behind a new policy. Instead of blaming the previous government, it would be sensible to look at the pros and cons of what has been done before and why the new policy would be better. If the government has an overriding objective, as it does now, which is to go for growth, the new policy should explain how that objective will be affected. This information should be clearly accessible in a podcast or on the gov.uk website. That would not change the policy, but it might well change the public's attitude to the government.

This is all I advocate doing immediately, as it would take quite a time for these changes to bed down. I belive they would send out a clear message to citizens that those who govern are compassionate, are applying common sense and are following the logic of their own declared policy of growth and improved productivity. The message is also that for a 'growth' scenario, it is better to tax consumption than tax the cost of employing people to achieve that growth. The overall effect of these changes should radically change the public's perception of what is really meant by a growth strategy and restore public confidence to spend and service industries to invest.

The whole question of UKCG debt and how to reduce it is discussed in Part 2 of this book. The overall short term impact of these tax changes is covered in Chapter 13. The changes would have resulted in an immediate tax increase of just over half that proposed in the October '24 budget (now implemented). The psychological effect, particularly on business growth but also on citizens would likely be very positive, but impossible to quantify.

CHAPTER 3

Health and social care

| **Control** | Should UKG control this? | **YES** |
| **Manage** | Should UKG manage this? | **NO** |

GOVERNMENT EXPENDITURE IN 2024/25
OBR estimate £202 billion

UKCG must control this because of the obvious need to provide citizens with a national service which maintains physical and mental wellbeing in the form of hospitals and specialist medical centres, in order to have a healthy population.

Managing this however need not be the preserve of UKCG. At present UKCG manages the workforce and pays the cost of treatment, mostly free, within the National Health Service (NHS). This is unique in the developed world; other advanced countries provide a combination of central government funding and private health insurance (PHI). The estimated UKCG health expenditure this financial year ending April 2025 is £202 billion. The most recent estimate for private care cost was around £48 billion spent by the public in 2024, making the total about £250 billion, equivalent to £3,600 per person per annum.

My general principle for reform is that those people who can afford to buy PHI and companies that can afford or wish to buy PHI for their staff be encouraged to do so. PHI does not and should not cover Accident and Emergency where everyone must be treated equally without cost in order of need, as now.

The logic for PHI is to ask the wealthy, who already pay tax towards the funding of the NHS, to help pay for the extra staff and facilities needed to clear the seven million people on the waiting list for diagnosis and treatment, and to provide some headroom to pay competitive wages to doctors and nurses to try to avoid existing NHS staff leaving for better salaries elsewhere.

The NHS would remain of course, but the funding of it should be by a combination of all taxpayers and the health insurance companies.

THE PROBLEMS

The present system is not able to achieve its purpose. There is a shortage of key staff at all levels of expertise in the NHS and social care. There is a huge waiting list, about seven million, awaiting treatment or assessment. There are a reported 2.8 million people on long term sick leave as at December 2024. According to the British Medical Association*, mental illness (mainly anxiety and depression) now affects 19% of the working population (age 16-64), affects one in four of the 17-19 age group and one in six of the 7-16 age group (this latter situation has major implications for the UKCG Department for Education, covered in Chapter 8).

As this is the first Ministry where the need is control only, it has to be said that is does seem unreasonable to expect UKCG personnel based mainly in London to be able to manage the three million people (nearly 10% of the UK workforce) in the NHS and social care across the whole of the UK; since, in practice, the NHS is run by Hospital Chief Executives reporting to the Department of Health. This is a similar situation in education, where thousands of schools report to the DfE. There is a need to put a management layer in between the regions and the centre to carry out the implementation of UKCG policy effectively.

* bma.org.uk/advice-and-support/nhs-delivery-and-workforce/pressures/
nhs-backlog-data-analysis

Effective management needs to be close to customer needs and experience. In the private sector, incompetence is not usually tolerated for long, whereas in the public sector, it rarely results in job termination at all. Competence is essential in the NHS, where human survival can be at stake. But there have been a number of cases recently, Birmingham and Nottingham hospitals for example, where it seems incompetence has been covered up or tolerated.

The NHS has naturally found the need to meet budgetary constraints and a high level of diagnosis and treatment. Sadly, this is likely to always be the case, as some treatments and new research discoveries are very expensive to incorporate within the NHS nationally. In practice, the NHS is already reliant on the private sector in the form of the drugs and machinery used, equipment and hospital construction, facilities and maintenance.

The fundamental flaw in UKCG control is that supply of care is not meeting demand. In practice, the seven million people on the NHS waiting list means UKCG control is not working. Other European countries, such as France and Germany, have a mixture of public and private insurance funding for health treatment, so we are unique in universal free treatment. We can learn from their experience.

In general, physical problems are often resolved by one-off procedures, whereas mental health procedures are in effect, more subjective, requiring frequent appointments and taking more time to resolve. The restorative techniques within mental health are many and varied and require specialists in psychology, psychiatry or therapy. Physical health appointments are nearly always attended by the patient: that is far from the case with mental health patients which is disruptive for GP and hospital practitioners.*/**

* 'Patients miss about 20% of scheduled appointments for mental health treatment, almost twice the rate in other medical specialties.' Cambridge University Press report, 2018

In 2023/24 the Health and Safety Executive reported 50.8 million working days were lost due to illness, of which 17.1 million were for mental health reasons (mainly stress, depression and anxiety). The impact on business potential and therefore growth is obvious, and many of those off sick undoubtedly have specialist skills not easily replaced.

SHORT TERM SOLUTIONS
I   Funding
In the first instance, a start should be made to relieve UKCG of the current pressure on NHS spending, by recommending the cost of insuring private healthcare be covered initially by the biggest companies. The cost of this per month should be no greater than £300 per person at today's prices (it is 300 Euros in Germany). Companies with a turnover of say £1 billion or more should be encouraged to provide private healthcare for all their employees, and that cost should continue to be deductible from profits.

In theory, that would cost UKCG in corporation tax, but in practice that would be more than offset by the NHS benefitting from extra funding in the private sector, which is already helping the NHS to take up some of the excess demand at NHS hospitals. It would also create pressure for some other companies to do likewise to attract the best staff. This strategy would only accelerate what is already rapidly happening in the UK. I envisage that private funding would initially take up the slack to allow the NHS waiting list to gradually come down to near zero. Once that is embedded, the NHS would treat PHI patients the same as non-PHI patients, simply asking PHI patients for evidence of PHI cover from their insurance company.

** Cambridge University Press report 2018 Why don't patients attend their appointments? Maintaining engagement with psychiatric services | Advances in Psychiatric Treatment | Cambridge Core

Increasing privatisation is happening now because the NHS cannot cope with present demand on the present funding. The process of reducing the current waiting list will be of benefit to citizens who will be able to get back to their normal lives, to work and earning again more quickly.

2   Separate physical health from mental health

Physical health is already split between dentistry, physiology and ophthalmic treatment and the rest. There is also a tendency for specific treatments to be privatised. Local surgeries, for example, may advise you to go to Specsavers to de-wax your ears. There is no reason I can see why mental health cannot be separated off in order to provide greater focus on satisfying the current high need for help, particularly voiced by parents and carers of young people. This separation would initially centre around NHS CAMHS (Child and Adolescent Mental Health Services). I am not suggesting that mental health support of every kind needs to be privatised, although many of the professionals involved, such as educational psychologists, operate privately.

Rationale

To begin with, I cannot stress too highly the importance of UKCG helping to de-stress the population at large when it claims that it needs to impose extra taxes on the population or cut public spending. Such announcements are rarely followed by an explanation of the necessity to do so, in the context of growth, debt reduction or whatever hoped for benefit is driving the decision. Instead, 'bad news' tends to be dumped onto the public without hope or promise for the future. If the benefit is unclear, perhaps the policy is wrong: and this approach leads to increased stress and dissatisfaction, further undermining the positive context needed for growth.

As a former CEO in the private sector, if I had bad news to

deliver I would always explain the remedy to counteract it and relate some positive news about the future of the business at the same time, to assure the team that there would be a brighter outcome and what that would look like. At least those affected by the bad news had a context for a degree of hope, to enable them to re-engage, however reluctantly. I recommend UKCG takes a similar approach.

Secondly, in times of hardship especially, UKCG is courting disapproval and rejection if its actions disadvantage the poorest in our society. If policies involve suffering for the population, as a result of spending cuts on public services for example, it is surely best to ensure that they don't make the lives of people with the most needs, such as state reliant pensioners, families below the poverty line, children in care, the genuinely sick, disabled people and those needing and attending to full time care, suffer those cuts as well, or more so. Doing so exacerbates and emphasises just how unequal such people are, and means more people are likely to become mentally unwell.

Thirdly, the mental health need in the UK is obvious following the COVID outbreak and its effect on the lives of the whole population. A separate institutional approach would enable better focus on whether the issue is clinical or relational. An initial relational problem can become a clinical one. Worry can become stress, which can cause depression.

Mental health can also suffer in young people as a result of anxiety, bereavement of parent or friend, abuse, neglect or sudden traumatic event. Clearly there are some medical conditions which can also affect child and adult mental health such as cancer, thyroid, hormonal and neurological problems, vitamin deficiencies and so on, or there may be underlying learning disabilities or neurodiversity, to name a few issues. The involvement of clinical professionals in assessing the potential for self-harm, suicide or harm to others is also increasingly important, due in part at least to the potentially harmful effects of social media on these issues. Mental health assessments require empathy, compassion and a deep understanding of information concerning the circumstances and personal background of the individual.

Young people and mental health

The issues surrounding mental health are complex. There are effectively three stages of concern for young people - an initial parent/carer and/or schoolteacher concern via GPs and A&E, a transfer by school or local authority to an appraisal by an educational psychologist or a social worker, and finally a possible referral for a full clinical assessment involving psychiatrists and psychologists.

A social worker, when appropriate, will be one of the links with CAMHS if it is considered that further professional help is needed. This process already involves a great deal of information being passed between three UKCG departments, Department of Education, Department of Local Communities and Department of Health, each with their own budget restraints. This is in itself a reason for focusing on mental health separately, as the mental health of young people requires a cross-service unified response for which a separate budget should be applied at each stage.

Intervention at an early non-clinical stage, particularly in the case of schoolchildren, should be relational. Relational interventions are even more subjective than clinical or physical interventions. The National Institute for Health and Excellence (NICE) approves a variety of therapies for anxiety, depression and post-traumatic stress in particular but by no means every model of therapeutic intervention provided by the market, some of which might be extremely beneficial. That means UKCG must accept, as did the Blair Labour Government earlier this century, that 'what works' in relational therapy is what should be tried.

At the moment, the only measure used by UKCG for social workers having to support young people suffering from stress, abuse, neglect or acute anxiety is the Strengths and Difficulties Questionnaire (SDQ): any intervention that correlates to that benchmark ought to be approved and tried at school first before resorting to clinically labelling a child.

In conclusion

Every UK adult citizen has a certain level of insecurity and it would be surprising if children don't; but that does not mean they have a mental health problem. It's a question of how far along a spectrum a child is: in my view, it's likely that with appropriate relational support, the majority of issues can be effectively resolved either naturally at home or professionally in school. With a separate Mental Health service, better joined up services (called for by every inquiry into the tragic deaths of far too many children) and targeted support would underpin early intervention, preventing short term concerns becoming long term issues, severing the infamous school to prison pipeline (*see* Chapter 8, Education) and enabling all our children and young people to have healthy, enjoyable and satisfying lives.

3   More privately run alternatives to the NHS for minor treatments

I propose that a UKCG master franchise be established for minor injuries and procedures, all of which would be handled by qualified nurses and pharmacists. UKCG would appoint a team of senior physicians and specialists to oversee the master franchise permitted 'menu' of products and procedures, which would define those (products and procedures) which could be handled by commercially run new or existing minor injury or illness clinics and pharmacies, staffed by professionally qualified and competent people. Pricing would be a commercial decision for the retail outlet. Many of the procedures are minor and the cost is unlikely to be greater than the loss of earnings incurred through waiting in an NHS queue. These existing and new retail outlets should also have a 50% reduction in business rates organised, as it is currently for charity shops, which normally have an 80% reduction.

4   Do not reduce benefits for those most in need of support
UKCG welfare and benefit payments should not be reduced for people with genuinely serious difficulties and needs, particularly whilst the NHS is in crisis, or to put citizens in need below the poverty line (defined as 60% of the national average wage). At the same time, clearly there are fraudulent benefit claims at the moment, and these should be identified more rigorously than hitherto and fines imposed on the perpetrators. Figures published by the Department for Work and Pensions (DWP) show that in 2023/24 £7.4 billion was overpaid in benefits expenditure due to fraud.

CHAPTER 4

The law and access to it

Control	Should UKG control this?	**YES**
Manage	Should UKG manage this?	**NO**

As an independent country the UK is entitled to set down rules of behaviour for its citizens in order to protect their safety, both from each other and others beyond our borders. UKCG has to control what those laws are or will be, but cannot interfere with access to or attempt to control justice, currently the preserve of our Courts of Law. Clearly, if UKCG could overtly or secretly pervert the course of justice citizens will neither be safe nor feel safe.

PROBLEMS OF MANAGEMENT

Police numbers and prison capacity are insufficient to accommodate those convicted; concerningly, the size of our prison population and rate of imprisonment per capita is among the highest in Europe* and our recidivism rate is very high too: so many things are clearly seriously amiss. The Scandinavian countries have the best record regarding the size of the prison population and the best recidivism rates (ie the lowest), so we have something to learn from them.

At the same time, access to justice is not available to many citizens. Investigating domestic crime such as burglary, anti-social

* childrenofprisoners.eu/facts_and_figures/prisoners-total/

behaviour, stalking, domestic abuse, shoplifting are not seen as priorities, although they are priorities in ordinary people's lives. There is typically a huge delay in obtaining justice after the date of the crime or civil wrong.

SOLUTIONS

1   Increase police funding by 10%

The safety of citizens is one of the essential priorities for government, alongside health and a roof over our heads. This priority is met by the Home Office and the Ministry of Defence within UKCG. There were 235,000 full time equivalent police officers, support staff and community police officers as at 30th September 2024. Police annual funding for 2023/24* was £27.3 billion and should be increased by 10% to £30 billion immediately. The additional funding would add another 40,000 full time equivalent officers including community police officers across the major conurbations (where police strength is currently 250 officers or above per 100,000 people).

2   Focus on anti-social behaviour

The increased funding should focus on crimes which most affect ordinary citizens: domestic abuse and violence, burglary, anti-social behaviour, shoplifting, online abuse, scamming and so on. This would be a major contribution to growth, as local people and businesses would have a greater feeling of security if the problem of local and domestic crime were tackled more effectively.

*   gov.uk/government/statistics/police-funding-for-england-and-wales-2015-to-2025

3 Strengthen probation managed community service

As far as safely possible, involve offenders convicted of non-violent crimes in probation-managed community service (for example, within the RefreshingUK plan, described in Chapter 1). This would help reduce pressure on prison accommodation, savings from which would be reassigned to probation, provide skills training and might reduce recidivism.

4 Approve third party funding for civil class actions

Allow ordinary citizens affected by the same issue to combine and have their litigation funded by a third party to sue for justice, particularly if the defendant is a government owned institution or department, in order to save costs of prosecution and protect ordinary citizens from an injustice without compensation.

Following the PACCAR case in 2023,* the Supreme Court ruled that group litigation funding by a third party was unlawful. This meant that the well-known case of the *Postmasters and others vs the Post Office 2019* could not take place today in 2025, since funding group litigation, which itself oftens involves ordinary citizens wronged by large organisations or government agencies, is now no longer viable.

This is a fundamental barrier to justice for the ordinary citizen. In March 2024 the previous government sought to remedy this with the publication of the Litigation Funding Agreement (Enforceability) Bill but this has been abandoned by the present government. I strongly recommend that the Civil Justice Council, responsible for drafting the Bill, get this passed into law as soon as possible.

* supremecourt.uk/cases/uksc-2021-0078

5   More judges please!

We clearly need to invest in more judges and court availability to enable the public to seek justice more quickly. Doing so is a basic citizens' right and a founding principle of democracy which has been progressively eroded by successive governments over the last fifty years. The redress should be given second priority after health.

The shortage of judges is particularly acute within the family courts with London the most affected. In 2024, according to a National Audit Office report, settlement of cases, many of which concern protecting children from harm, took twice as long as the statutory 26 weeks maximum requirement. Furthermore, in 40% of cases the applicant or respondent had no legal representation: due, presumably, to the cost of funding being too great or non-availability of legal aid. The report also stressed that early intervention to protect children from harm would help reduce such cases (*see* Chapter 8, Education).

6   Citizens' Advice needed on legal rights

For citizens who may be rightly or wrongly arrested and questioned by the police during an incident, it would be helpful to know that they were entitled to free legal advice before questioning. That and other information including access to legal aid could be made clear at the website citizensadvice.org.uk, a familiar place where people seek useful information.

7   Fair pay for legal aid lawyers

Enforce legal aid provision by ensuring lawyers are adequately paid to represent citizens whose claims exceed £1,000.

8   Clarify income levels for legal aid

It should be made clear what income level justifies a claim for legal aid. With regard to seeking legal aid support for costs in relation to defending an action from a third party, such as a business, individual or government agency, the situation is often not made at all clear. For example, if your washing machine explodes and you are unable to obtain compensation from either the retailer or the manufacturer, will you be able to recover costs and a new machine if you sue the retailer and you are a pensioner? At present it is difficult to know the answer without going through an elaborate application procedure or having a conversation with the Citizens' Advice Bureau. It should be published online, if necessary using everyday examples.

9   Concentrate far more on prison reform

There needs to be a far greater concentration on rehabilitation and re-integration into UK society of individuals both within prison itself and upon discharge. Addressing the high incidence of dyslexia, illiteracy and trauma amongst the prison population would be steps in the right direction.

By comparison to Norway the UK system focuses purely on punishment and retribution. UK prisons are also overcrowded and the staff to prisoner ratio is low compared to Norway.

Attempts were made in 2023 to try to alleviate the pressure on prison overcrowding by renting space in prisons oversees in the Netherlands and Belgium, something Norway had experimented with previously. But the conclusion of Norway by 2020 was that this did not help. The solution in the UK would be to build more open regional prisons, increase the staff to prisoner ratio and focus on creating as normal a daily routine as feasible, including more constructive attitude towards reducing the recidivism rate which remains very high in the UK compared to most other developed countries.

10   Combat adolescent crime with earlier interventions

UKCG needs to combat the increasing number of teenage children being arrested for notifiable offences with a particular concern being related to knife crime. Offending in general is at its highest at 18-20 years old. According to Youth Justice Board statistics* published in January 2025 for the year ending 2024, 32.5% of children released reoffended. Equally, the National Education Union (NEU) are concerned about teenage violence against teaching staff in school today.**

A way to address these horrifying statistics is to focus on helping the most vulnerable children as early as possible in their early school life by the Department of Education placing a far greater emphasis, through Ofsted, on the importance of supporting children, particularly boys (96% of the UK prison population was male in June 2024), who are subjected to home abuse, neglect or abnormal disruption in their early lives and including them in the classroom rather than excluding them. Boys are 1.5 times more likely to be excluded than girls, particularly between the ages of 12 to 15.*** Once children are on the street instead of at school, they are more vulnerable to drug traffickers and child abusers. This subject is covered in detail in Chapter 8.

The cumulative effect of all these measures should be a major positive impact on growth, as our streets and homes become and feel safer. And if the inordinate amount of time spent by authorities and by the public in seeking redress from wrong is reduced, it can be far better spent at work or at leisure.

---

* gov.uk/government/statistics/youth-justice-statistics-2023-to-2024/youth-justice-statistics-2023-to-2024

** Violence in the education sector | National Education Union

*** explore-education-statistics.service.gov.uk/

CHAPTER 5

Defence

Control	Should UKG control this?	**YES**
Manage	Should UKG manage this?	**YES**

Only UKCG can hope to ensure citizen safety from an attack by a foreign power. Only UKCG can manage that reality.

THE PROBLEM

We are a small country and have less weapons of defence or attack than many other countries, including potentially aggressive ones. It is impossible to know what will be needed to defend our citizens and when. We also need to defend against random cyber-attack as well as physical attack, and sabotage of offshore facilities such as undersea cables.

The English Channel used to be our defence against all but major air attack: now drones and digital interference make that irrelevant. In modern warfare missile attack is common and missile speed and range is constantly being increased. The UK defence against missile attack is weak. The UK does not have US made Patriot missile defence system compared to some other NATO countries such as Germany or the Netherlands. The US Patriot missile defence system is a minimum cost of US $1.5 billion and a lot more to retain. As far I am aware there is no UK defence against hypersonic (five times the speed of sound or more) missiles. Although the UK has a deterrent nuclear armed submarine, I assume there is no defence to nuclear attack, since presumably we would have been obliterated before reaction was possible.

We are reliant for defence on the USA. However there is no reason to believe that the USA will always fight the Eurozone battles. We also use the army as a back-up to policing.

SOLUTIONS

I   Increase the size of the army

In April 2024 the number of people in our armed forces was about 148,000 excluding reserves, of which 5,700 were stationed overseas. There has been a decline in the proportion of total personnel working within the army from 61% in 2012 to 56% in 2024, and a gradual decline in manpower over the last twelve years.

The army needs to increase from 82,000 to 100,000 full time soldiers. This is for two reasons:

i)   because the army is currently the most significant factor in keeping people safe in the current war in Ukraine, and will remain so in any future conflict that involves territorial seizure or defence support for overseas allies.

ii) the army is needed as a back-up to policing which is likely to be increasingly needed in future in response to natural disasters, caused by yet more challenging climate change.

Such an increase will take time to achieve.

2   Invest in a missile defence shield

Increasing defence spending to 2.5% of GDP does not take into account the cost of a missile defence shield which is essential for securing the safety of UK citizens at the moment: whereas an increase to 3% of GDP would. This is an extra capital expenditure of £15 billion, where the financial return becomes irrelevant whilst the threat of a European war persists.

3   Promote venture capital for cyber-defence

UKCG venture capital should support new and existing defence-based software and hardware companies to develop our capacity to respond to attack through the use of such drones and cybersecurity measures as might be required for both our armed forces and the secret services.

4   Clarify priorities

The above should take priority over other major air and sea multi-billion pound projects which inevitably become modified by technological advance over time and take many years to complete.

5   Increase the Defence budget

Whilst we rely on the USA and its membership of the North Atlantic Treaty Organisation (NATO) for the ultimate deterrent to enemy aggression, we should ensure we spend an appropriate proportion of GDP (currently 2.3% according to recent government announcements) on defence, which now needs to be 3%. The cost of this is likely to be around £21 billion, mainly for missile defence, on top of the current 2024/25 expenditure of around £65 billion. This is a very substantial sum which will require serious savings from other UKCG departments (*see* Chapter 13). This investment will benefit companies like BAE Systems plc, our major defence systems supplier, which will doubtless also benefit from the renewed European interest in defence as well, both of which will help growth in the next few years.

6   Defence treaty with Europe

If not already completed by the publication of this book, UKCG needs to have a defence treaty with the European Union which covers all forms of defence and information sharing required to protect UK and European citizens.

7   Ensure availability of key defence components

One other form of defence less usually discussed is UKCG's need to continue to have access to the components essential for making high tech items such as drones, as well as machines/technology critical to modern warfare (computers, batteries and electronic connection devices such as fibre optic cables).

For example, Taiwan has a near monopoly of the most sophisticated microchips and the USA, with its ultra-pure quartz mines in North Carolina, has a similar control of semiconductors made from that rock. Rare earth minerals (hard to separate from rock, thus making them 'rare') are a vital ingredient of smart phones, computers and the equipment built to relay information through undersea fibre optic cables. Greenland and Ukraine have large deposits, which may explain why the current US President is interested in both.

Batteries are also essential in warfare and in electric vehicles (EVs), which use a huge amount of copper. Panama has one of the largest copper mines in the world, but it is currently closed and in need of investment. Both the USA and China are focussed on and involved there. UKCG and Europe need battery production factories, within Europe, but preferably not financed by China which now controls nearly 90% of EV battery supply through their ownership of cobalt and lithium mining rights, key to battery creation.

All these things are warning signs for UKCG when it comes to effective defence: that it must ensure future availability of key components. Expenditure on defence will obviously create growth for those companies able to supply all or part of the resources listed, many of which are in the UK. There may also be European export value in such UK production too.

CHAPTER 6

Housing and land use

CONTROL	Should UKCG control this?	**YES**
MANAGE	Should UKCG manage this?	**NO**

UKCG must control the availability of land for house building through the planning system, which it already controls. Local Authorities are responsible for building control (essentially safety of construction) but this is not always done well (the fire risk cladding disaster at Grenfell Tower in London being an obvious example).

UKCG is unable to manage this because it relies on the cooperation of many different organisations and people both in the UK and overseas to construct any form of safe housing.

THE PROBLEM

There is insufficient housing to rent. Those wanting to own houses cannot afford to do so. There are therefore too many homeless people, including those in insecure and temporary housing. Since a roof over our heads is one of the basic necessities for all of us, this has to be a high priority issue.

The rate of housebuilding is under the control of the private sector, not UKCG. There is already planning permission for building UKCG's stated target of 1.5 million new homes over five years, but that target is irrelevant since the private sector has several constraints.

The main constraints are:

- The availability and cost of labour and building components
- The need to retain a land bank of approved planning permission sites for the long term survival of the main builders which are public companies with shareholders, including pension funds
- The need to build a price range of houses or flats to ensure profitability rather than just low-cost units.

The effect of increasing the planning approval to build on more land is good for the long term survival of builders but has to be viewed in the context of building land being finite within the overall assessment of what should constitute green areas, compared to brown areas. The higher the perceived need to retain green areas, the greater the need to build high rise blocks of flats to house our increasing population.

SOLUTIONS

I   Opening the housing market for first time buyers through a new form of shared property ownership

The average price (to the nearest thousand) of a dwelling in the UK in November 2024 according to the Land Registry was £306,000 in England, £219,000 in Wales and £195,000 in Scotland and Northern Ireland, an overall average of £267,000. The average full time gross annual salary was £37,000. Mortgage lenders are unlikely to lend more than five times gross salary, so using these average salary and house price figures, a buyer would need to borrow seven times salary or find a £82,000 deposit and borrow at least five times their salary.

Therefore, my solution is to create a tradeable stock market option for the landlord's share of a shared ownership domestic property. I also propose to remove inflation from the rent payable proportion.

This is a radical proposal which would dramatically increase home ownership, particularly for young people.

UKCG already has a good range of share ownership options, but they mostly refer to leasehold properties. I would open new build and existing properties to be sold as share ownership as well as outright sale where the need arises - this need would be provided by an open market. In shared ownership, there are basically three agreements:

    i)   one to purchase a share

    ii)   one to cover staircasing which is the option to buy, in stages or outright, the remaining share of what now would be a freehold property

and

    iii)   one to cover the rental agreement to protect the landlord.

As of now, the buyer (a first-time buyer initially but the scheme could be extended to any buyer) can obtain a mortgage from a reputable lender for a share of a shared ownership property. However, the existing UKCG process applies inflation to the basic rent, usually commencing at 2.75-3% of the residual property value not acquired by the buyer. Although that inflation is capped by a further 1% maximum on the base level, the base of it, the consumer price index, is hugely variable. My proposal is to fix that rent for life at a maximum level of 3% of the residual freehold value at the time of purchase. As with all current shared ownership government schemes, being able to staircase any number of times is essential. But I would propose a minimum staircase payment of £1,000.

There should be a ready market, including UK pension funds, for the landlord's residual share in a property under the shared ownership scheme. This is because in addition to a 3% regular return on the original remaining shareholding, the property value itself will be increasing over time. Also under the landlord agreement the landlord would have repossession rights if the original purchaser failed to pay the rent for a six-month period. The original purchaser will also be able to sell their original investment in the property plus inflation and may well find the landlord a competitive sale source option, in other words, interested in buying that proportion themselves.

2   A new local authority rent guarantor scheme

I advocate widespread introduction of a new limited rent guarantor scheme for tenants that favours local authorities (LAs) which, in their allotted area, have responsibility for the homeless, looked after children aged between 18 and 25 and those who need housing but cannot afford it.

I propose two separate schemes, one for short term rental where the LA rent guarantee would last for three years only, and one for new build-to-rent housing where the LA rent guarantee would be for seven years.

I know from experience that investors in social housing would accept a suitably worded LA seven-year rent guarantee as a basis for a new build development by the private sector. I use the word 'limited' for the guarantee, as the total amount of financial exposure for the LA would be limited to an agreed level in advance for the sums for the rent cost over three years or seven years and the estimate of repairs which could be incurred beyond routine wear and tear in that period. The limited guarantee would be off LA balance sheet, and the actual cost crystallised if and when it occurred.

The three year guarantee could operate immediately. LAs willing to embrace the scheme would provide estate agencies in their area with details of the guarantee being offered. This would result in the LA gaining priority for the people in the most need from estate agents: greater acceptance of vulnerable tenants by local landlords: and greater interest (amongst landlords) in making property available for those in most need. There is such a scheme available at present which has not been adopted as yet by LAs.

CHAPTER 7

Energy supply

Control	Should UKG control this?	**YES**
Manage	Should UKG manage this?	**NO**

The UKCG needs to ensure that the lights don't go out in the UK by controlling the storage, amount and source of energy purchased from a choice of fossil fuels and alternative renewable energy sources of supply. There is no necessity and no possibility for UKCG to manage the process of supply of energy which comes from disparate and worldwide sources, is in abundant supply and traded on international wholesale markets.

THE PROBLEMS

The objective of net zero, where the output of green house gases is equalled by the cancellation impact of emissions removed from the atmosphere, is creating a problem for UKCG because the cost of investing in and exploiting the availability of renewable energy sources will have to be paid by the tax paying consumer in their bills. This is restricting growth by increasing business costs and reducing consumer spending power. If all other nations applied the same tax charges as UKCG for investing in renewables it would be less of a problem, but that is not currently the case.

Currently UKCG imports 37% of its energy supply in the form of gas. There is general agreement that fossil fuels should be phased out as an energy source, but no agreement on when. There does not appear to be a clear investment strategy for obtaining replacement for gas energy sources. Wind and solar power are the most easily obtained major renewable energy sources for the UK, but the cost of connecting them to the National Grid is extremely high. At the moment there is also inadequate storage of fossil fuels during the transition to renewables. The lack of investment in storage of renewable energy resources remains a problem. At the time of writing, there is no clear policy for nuclear energy.

As at June 2024 according to figures recently published by UKCG,* petrol prices were reasonably compatible with European countries, but pricing of diesel fuel used by commercial as well as domestic vehicles was the second highest in Europe. At the same time, electricity costs in the UK were around 27 pence per kilowatt hour compared to the EU14 country median of 14 pence, about twice as high. Consumers in the UK already pay more than industrial users; for electricity 25% more and gas 60% more. The UK consumer subsidy for renewables in those costs is the highest percentage in the EU14 and partly explains why our energy costs in UK are expensive in relation to Europe.

With regard to storage and distribution of energy resources, fossil fuel distribution is well established but is causing global warming. Batteries are the best form of electrical storage. The reliability, cost, storage and means of national distribution of renewable sources of energy remain unresolved issues at the moment.

* Comparisons of international road fuel prices - gov.uk

SOLUTIONS

I   Be more realistic about taxpayer funding of net zero

Although unpopular and problematic for many citizens, the present UKCG policy of consumer subsidy of the switch to net zero is the right one, for the sake of the younger generation. The actual cost of electricity can be reduced through the introduction of some new measures without affecting that principle. It would help if UKCG explained to the population the long term damage that would result from not taking these steps. Furthermore, a lack of appropriate action would badly affect citizen's main assets, and cost the younger generation a lot more in the future than their parents today if not implemented now.

Requiring UK citizens to pay for reducing emissions by 68% by 2030 as UKCG agreed to do at the Paris Agreement in 2015 (COP21) however, is simply impossible. It would require 20% of households to have heat pumps by then, all cars being electric, together with many other actions as yet not legislated for. It is inconceivable that citizens could afford to pay for such dramatic action in so short a time, however desirable it might be. Allowing 20 years for citizens to pay to make the transition to net zero is still demanding, but more realistic. In their latest report (February 2025), the Climate Change Committee has already stated that the 2030 target will not be met by some margin, and citizens are already struggling to pay high energy bills. So in addition to the recommendations of the Climate Change Committee* within a revised time frame, we can also look at the following measures to meet the new target of 2045.

*   The Seventh Carbon Budget - Climate Change Committee

2   Store more gas reserves

Since gas still forms a major part of energy supply it would be sensible to store more gas reserves. We store about 2% of our needs compared to about 25% in Europe. With greater storage there is more time to take advantage of occasions of relatively lower wholesale prices and more time to avoid paying very high prices on the markets. This should contribute to lower energy prices for consumers. It is also a hedge against unexpected political interference in overseas gas supply.

3   Split wholesale renewables pricing from fossil fuels

We should try to change the way wholesale electricity prices, on which UK retail energy suppliers rely for their retail pricing, are controlled by the highest price of gas being supplied, as they are currently. This is a complex issue on its own but would save households in particular a lot of money if that control was changed. The obvious solution would be to separate wholesale prices of fuels from renewables. It should be an urgent consideration for the new UKCG Energy Fund to address and try to effect.

4   Retain existing fossil fuel approvals

We should allow the existing exploratory UKCG controlled gas approvals to remain and not be revoked. We still need gas at the moment, and it is cheaper and likely less carbon emitting to use our own than import it (currently some is brought to the UK from Peru).

5   Explore hydrogen potential

We should fully explore the potential of hydrogen in the quest for alternatives to fossil fuels. Toyota and Hyundai already have hydrogen cell driven cars and JC Bamford are using hydrogen for their commercial vehicles where admittedly the fuel storage tanks can be bigger. There is even a hydrogen driven train in the UK.* In the USA the previous Biden administration released a strategy and roadmap for exploiting hydrogen as an ecologically beneficial energy source in June 2023, and UKCG should do the same. The distribution and storage of hydrogen envisaged by British Gas should be supported.**

6   Be honest about the impact of pylons

Relying on renewables in the future means we must be honest about the impact of pylons in the UK. The renewable energy delivery mechanism chosen for wind power is the pylon. According to National Grid, onshore pylon delivery is cheaper than offshore pylon delivery or underground cabling. That means that the UK population is assumed to have decided to tolerate a large increase in pylons rather than have higher energy bills. Where those new pylons will be, and what they will look like, will have an impact on where housing development should be. It would be sensible for everyone to be able to see a pylon grid map to understand what is happening and being proposed. The future network blueprint is available from National Grid now: a statement of what has been agreed and funded should be published clearly online in order that everyone in the UK knows what to expect.

7   Minigrids as well as National Grid

We should also investigate establishing mini regional grids. Such grids contain the option to be connected or disconnected to the National Grid so would be particularly useful for local energy

---

 *   porterbrook.co.uk/innovation/hydroflex
 ** telegraph.co.uk/business/2024/10/19/british-gas-giant-unveils-60-mile-blue-hydrogen-pipeline/

conservation as well as national supply. There will clearly be areas in the UK with greater natural renewable energy resources than others, whether that be hydro, solar or wind.

8   Explore effective battery storage

Cost effective lead battery storage* from renewables, such as solar panels or a small wind turbine and generator at individual household properties or for small local areas should be explored and implemented with UKCG support if that is cheaper for citizens, in order to reduce the national installation of unsightly pylons.

9   No nuclear investment

I can see no point in pursuing a nuclear based strategy since the investment is huge and takes many years to build, is an obvious target for an enemy in wartime, and radiation leaks and their prevention remain a concern.

---

*   batterycouncil.org/

CHAPTER 8

Education and inclusion

| **Control** | Should UKG control this? | **YES** |
| **Manage** | Should UKG manage this? | **NO** |

Every UK child should receive an education, and UKCG requires parents/carers, schools and the school staff to ensure all children do so. UKCG also needs to ensure that children can be educated to a certain universally recognised standard by suitably educated teachers. The standard would be represented by the content and degree of difficulty of the examination questions and other benchmarking criteria, which UKCG should control.

As is the case for health, there is no practical way UKCG can manage this process and no necessity to do so. The evidence will be in the exams results. At present UKCG use Ofsted to monitor progress, but currently that doesn't have the support of the teaching profession which rightly believes it knows better. Ideally parents, through governorship of schools, should root out incompetence rather than Ofsted.

However, the direct involvement of parents/carers with their children's school staff varies greatly across the UK, depending on the level of interest/capacity of the parent/carer and the extent to which a school seeks to involve the parent/carer in their child's progress at school. This is one of the differences between the private schooling system, where it is assumed that the parents have a great interest in their child's progress at school because they are paying for it, and the state system, which is free, and the parental approach is initially unknown. This arguably makes it harder for teachers in the state system to make progress with every child. As in the case for health, there must be an alternative privately funded source for children to be well educated if the system currently reporting to the Department for Education (DfE) is failing to educate every pupil. But such privilege is currently largely confined to parents who can afford it and is therefore by no means a complete solution to guaranteeing a high educational standard of pupil performance and opportunity for all.

THE PROBLEMS

The control and management of education and educational standards is currently a mess from a UKCG standpoint. About 80% of state secondary schools and about 50% of state primary and nursery schools are called academies, which report to the Department for Education (DfE). The remaining schools, mainly called community schools, report to the government local authority (LA) which reports to the Minister for Housing, Communities and Local Government (MHCLG).

Thus there are two separate departments with different objectives. However, educational standards are affected by the mental health of children and their parents/carers, amongst other factors, and whether all children are attending school. If children are excluded from school or fail to attend school, the cost of caring for them passes to MHCLG. It is in the interests of the DfE to maximise good exam results which tacitly leads to school exclusion of disruptive children: and in the MHCLG's interest to maximise inclusion and attendance at school. Ofsted works for the DfE with the purpose of raising the educational standard, not the behavioural standard of children.

This schism in departmental approaches is further exacerbated by the decision in 2010 to create Virtual Schools which now have the responsibility to support children looked after in the care system, those who are adopted, fostered, have a social worker or are in some form of kinship care, representing about 5% of children of school age. The Virtual Schools also have a budget from MHCLG, but of course are unable to fully implement their policy of providing mental health support and advice in schools controlled by the DfE, because that would cost the DfE more time and money and disrupt the aim of attaining the higher educational standard monitored by Ofsted. The DfE needs to incorporate the Virtual School perspective into Ofsted reports, otherwise it is questionable as to why there are Virtual School staff at all.

This mess has a huge impact on UKCG expenditure on special schools, on street crime from children not at school and vulnerable to abuse, grooming, organised crime and drug dealers, on children's homes, on the NHS for mental health treatment, on policing, and worst of all, on children and young people, already made the most vulnerable in our society through their early experiences, in dire need of help and support and not getting it.

UKCG has also decided to apply VAT to private school fees (but not to private health bills as previously stated) which has created greater pressure on the state system already suffering from teacher shortage, pupil mental health issues and absenteeism. According to the British Medical Association mental health issues currently affect 17% of 7-16-year-olds, and 25% of 17-19 year-olds.

Finally, and most importantly, in the last ten years there has been an increase in teacher vacancies to nearly 3,000 at the end of March 2024, a situation now made worse by the requirement to take on additional numbers of pupils who have left the private sector after the imposition of VAT. Teachers are also leaving in greater numbers each year due to excessive workload, poor pay and lack of support particularly in the field of challenging pupil behaviour.*

SOLUTIONS

1   Clarity of reporting

Make all schools report to one department, the DfE, which will need a bigger budget to deal with mental health issues at school (*and see also* Chapter 3). The increase will mainly be in training and salaries to cover extra time spent in helping children who are struggling to settle to learn but will represent savings in the middle to long term to the DfE as well as other Departments (*as above*).

2   Reintroduce Sure Start

Reintroduce the Sure Start Programme for up to four years olds as previously instigated by the Labour government in 1999. This would be far better that the proposed replacement today called Family Hubs and Start for Life which aims to cover all children. The Family Hubs have far too wide a brief, whereas Sure Start focused on the critical early years and readiness for primary school, has a proven track record of outstanding success and is a lot cheaper to fund. The existing surviving Sure Start Nursery schools should provide the basis for increased DfE funding here.

3   Involve the Virtual School earlier

Re-configure the criteria of Ofsted inspections to embrace the school's actual ability to support and help disadvantaged pupils by seeing evidence of that support working. Obtaining an opinion from the Virtual School, which should be mandatory before commencing a second suspension or final exclusion of a child from their school,

---

*   DfE, & Peirson-Hagger I Times Educational Supplement 2024

should be part of the Ofsted school report on safeguarding. If agreement cannot be reached, the case should go to tribunal. This will give the child concerned the protection of an outside voice focusing on wellness in general, rather than simply the view of the DfE reporting Head.

This is particularly sensitive and relevant for reporting on safeguarding boys in secondary school. Inclusion at this stage of education should be a high priority. The problems that occur from school exclusion of teenage boys (76% of exclusions are boys) are sadly reflected in teenage crime statistics and often reflect the damaged background that has affected those children. The zero tolerance school discipline policy that often leads to placement in young offender institutions, and children as young as 15 held on remand awaiting placement, should be replaced by a more considered and measured approach. The UKCG recent approval of using PAVA spray on children in those young offender institutions should be utterly condemned and reflects as much frustrated temper amongst adults as it does amongst the children and young people, whose relational needs have likely not as yet been adequately recognised and met.

4   Regional monitoring

Monitor the success of schools on a regional basis rather than a national one, with a review body for wellbeing as well academic experts, in order to take into account regional differences.

5   Managing failing schools

If possible when necessary, replace a school head in a 'failing' school with another from the same region who has been successful across the new criteria.

6   Budget increase needed

Increase the DfE budget from £61.6 billion to £63 billion for 2025/26. There will be difficulties in quantifying savings in the MHCLG budget in the short term if my recommendations were followed on early intervention on behalf of disadvantaged pupils, but they should be substantial enough to offset the budget increase.

7   Include all children

Make it clear that all schools have a responsibility to educate all children however challenging they might be and that exclusion and/or suspension from school must be an exceptionally rare occurrence. In the year ending March 2024, pupil suspensions increased 40% over the previous year and exclusions increased by 34%. Pupil persistent absentee percentage (misses 10% or more of their scheduled school sessions within an academic year) remains at around 20%. Early intervention and pupil support at primary level is crucial and the most effective long term for struggling pupils and their families.

8   Expand the Virtual School brief

Change the Virtual School brief to include supporting the parents of all children likely to be excluded where necessary, as well as the carers of looked after children, kinship carers and parents of children with social workers whom they already support. Virtual schools could also be tasked to advise on reducing absenteeism.

9   Therapeutic support from the Virtual School

With immediate effect, allow Virtual School Heads the right to determine a menu of therapeutic help for pupils a school wishes to suspend or exclude, for which the school must allocate adequate resources, funded by the DfE. This would need to be in conjunction with recommendation 8 above. Wherever possible, Virtual School staff would be full time, to provide continuity of relationship for children, families and staff, the bedrock of security and wellbeing.

10 Use software to lower EHCP costs

The cost of EHCPs (Education and Health Care Plans) should be reduced and improved by requiring schools to use existing software which incorporates pupil home and school background, pupil's needs and profile, attendance, advice of a social worker or educational psychologist if appropriate, evidence of the actions school has taken to help the pupil and the results of those actions. This would bring professionals together, providing consistency of approach within the Teams around the child: it would also help reduce the number of those on an exclusion pathway by holding staff accountable for early intervention and for creating the appropriate environment for the child. This would also have the impact of reducing costs of identifying those who need an EHCP, and providing the resources required by one.

11 Growth as a discussion topic in school

Introduce the subject of growth and productivity as part of the PHSE curriculum from year 7. This would create discussions on what can be done, what should not be done, and whether growth is, overall, the right objective. Subjects could include *"What do you want out of life?"*, *"What do you want to contribute?"* *"What would you need to help you to contribute?"* and so on. This subject may well resonate particularly with disadvantaged children from whom school staff can learn, and help young people during the impending transition to adulthood.

12 Focus much more on teacher support

Within Ofsted inspections, there appears to be little credence placed on the importance of a relational policy within schools, and inadequate realisation from Government that teachers are suffering from work overload. Both these factors place undue pressure on classroom teaching.

There are a number of ways this can be addressed. The role of teaching assistants has always been helpful in supporting classroom teachers to develop relationships with pupils particularly when challenging behaviour disrupts class progress. This role has become sidelined in some schools, and that is wrong in my view. Teachers need time allocated to reflect on the relational problems they face with pupils. Educational psychologists or specialist members of the Virtual School team can contribute to supporting staff via reflective sessions online and in person.

Equally schools should invest more in relational and behavioural resources including online tools for staff to provide the 'wrap around' support that they, the teachers, and their pupils need. That investment will save future costs and help many teachers and students.

CHAPTER 9

Immigration
and emigration

Control	Should UKG control this?	**YES**
Manage	Should UKG manage this?	**YES**

UKCG needs to both control and manage the total number of people living in the UK for all the obvious reasons of ensuring that the needs of the population, including safety and the rule of law, are adequately met. However, UKCG obligations under international laws must also be met. To that extent UKCG cannot manage immigration or emigration alone.

THE PROBLEMS

People wishing to enter the UK permanently are normally divided into two categories:

- Those who have a legal right to stay (through acquiring citizenship, for example or have a legitimate visa to do so)
- Those who do not as yet have a legal right to stay, for example those who are seeking asylum from their country of birth due to war, famine, or those who simply have a desire to live here

There are also people who wish to live in the UK for part of the year or for a specific number of years for educational or employment reasons, such as students, seasonal workers and people we welcome on work visas for their skills. There should be no problem with specific individuals in this category.

With respect to people who arrive in the UK seeking sanctuary, the first issue to address is applying for asylum to the UK. Anyone already in the UK can apply for asylum. Anyone claiming asylum is protected under the 1951 Refugee Convention as modified in the 1967 protocol. 149 countries are signatories to this and the protocol, including the UK. This means that any 'safe' country, which essentially means a nation which would not return an individual to the country in which they claim they have been or would be persecuted, must consider a request for asylum, providing the person has not already been within a 'safe' country prior to arriving in the UK. A person fleeing a country who is not deemed by the UK after due legal process to have a valid reason to be given asylum here cannot be classed as a refugee.

However, in 2023, UKCG passed the Illegal Immigration Act. This act repudiated the Refugee Convention protocol by insisting that anyone who was not in the UK at the time the law was passed could not apply for asylum. If they subsequently arrive in the UK on a boat or aircraft and have previously been in a safe country (a fellow signatory of the Refugee Convention) they might not be granted asylum. The effect of this 2023 Act is to make anyone who applies for asylum who was not in the UK before the 2023 Act illegal applicants for asylum.

Despite this, it is still not clear exactly who could be correctly termed an 'illegal' immigrant because the UKCG current guidance implies a number of further enquiries needs to be made before defining 'illegal'.* This complexity gives rise to argument about who is an 'illegal' immigrant and who is a legal applicant for asylum. This position is further complicated by the unwillingness of European

---

* Claim asylum in the UK: Eligibility - gov.uk

'safe' countries who are the first port of call for asylum seekers to provide asylum in their country for some or all who arrive on boats. In theory, anyone who has already passed through a 'safe' country arriving in the UK is an illegal immigrant, under current UK law, as above, but human compassion ignores that proviso when presented with a boat arriving on UK shores full of real people.

The effect of the Illegal Immigration Act is actually to encourage illegal entry into the UK, because that overcomes the first objection of not being in the UK as the basis of an asylum claim. That creates greater pressure on handling immigrants who actually are here illegally (for example, those who have overstayed their visas or arrived without permission but are not claiming asylum, those whose asylum claims have been refused and who can be returned to their country, and so on).

There is a shortage of key workers in some important industries such as health and social care in the UK which need filling. There is also a need to welcome university students both to enhance our reputation as a good educator and to enable UK students to easily study abroad. Losing free movement of UK citizens throughout the European Union has created problems for UK companies and citizens. Policy towards legal and illegal immigrants lacks clarity, particularly when those here illegally (as described above) have skills we desperately need in the UK.

Finally, the birth rate (Total Fertility Rate TFR) in England and Wales fell to 1.44 births per woman in 2023 (the lowest since records began in 1938)* compared to a rate of at least 2 seen as the minimum level required to sustain the size of the population. This is a disturbing trend, shared with many nations, which will rapidly create an ageing UK population and a need for more full time workers.

* ons.gov.uk/peoplepopulationandcommunity/birthsdeathsandmarriages/ livebirths/bulletins/birthsummarytablesenglandandwales/2023

SOLUTIONS

I   Determine a realistic total population figure

It would be helpful to determine the maximum number of people we would accept in the UK for the time being. The number should be based on the support structures which exist for the current population. I would suggest the number would be 70 million based on the present level of resources (the actual population is estimated at 69.4 million (as at January 2025). The number can be changed when necessary but would provide a clear statement that once that level is reached, all further applicants for citizenship would be refused until that number reduces. In practice, about 480,000 people emigrated from the UK in 2023/24 so there would be theoretical room to replace them with immigrants should we choose to do so.

2   Clarify the legal basis for asylum

We need to clarify what would be a genuine legal basis for seeking asylum in the UK rather than the present phrasing we 'might' allow entry if an applicant has a legal basis. UKCG cannot continue to both support the Refugee Convention and legislate against that support. That is effectively promoting homelessness of citizens from other countries and is inhumane.

3   Restore some free movement

We need to agree with the EU the proposed free movement of young people on a visa basis to and from UK as a matter of urgency.

4   Oversea help from young people looking for opportunities in the UK

We have an existing Tier 1 and Tier 2 visa application system which promotes UK residency and, where appropriate, a route for applicants to achieve Indefinite Leave to Remain (ILR) status which can lead to citizenship if the conditions are met. The Tier 1 investor welcome aspect was eradicated by the previous government in 2022, but as far as I am aware the new business entrepreneurial interest remains for potential immigrants wishing to develop ideas and employ people in the UK.

The Tier 2 visas status is largely for those with essential skills that the UK needs. It would make sense to make it clear that we welcome those whose abilities or standing meet the tiered visa criteria, not least because of the declining availability of young people in the UK.

5   Work with Europe

Working through asylum applications from increasing numbers of asylum seekers is an issue affecting most of Europe, so the best solution to this problem would be a joint one with the other affected European countries. This is already being considered by UKCG.

6   Permit asylum seekers to work earlier

Asylum seekers should be able to seek work if their application is not handled within six months, rather than 12 months.

7   Expand the Immigration Salary List

The Immigration Salary List is too restrictive in defining job opportunities. With several million UK citizens unable to work through long term sickness, expanding the list would make sense.

CHAPTER 10

Transport in the UK

Control	Should UKG control this?	**YES**
Manage	Should UKG manage this?	**NO**

UKCG has to control the use of the land in the UK and therefore what transport links it has. Adding to the number and type of roads and the amount of rail track is therefore under UKCG control. Managing the use of transport links is not the preserve of UKCG on the roads or in the air (apart from a golden share in privately run air traffic control) and there is no necessity for it to be on the rails either.

THE PROBLEMS

There is no clear strategy regarding private/public ownership of the means of travel. Ownership of rail, airports and roads are all a mix of private/public ownership. This allows 'buck passing' whenever problems occur, leaving UK citizens with the problem and cost of disruption. The effects of climate change have not been clearly identified as a defining consideration in investing in networks now and in the future. The result has been confused policy thinking and inertia on decision making. Efficient transport is a vital aid to growth.

On UK railways, UKCG have experimented with privatising the rail network into regions for train investment and operation but not the maintenance of track or signalling, which remains in public ownership.

There are 29 UK international airports. Ownership of the 29 airports is 10.3% UKCG (represented by Cardiff, Inverness and Glasgow Prestwick), 26.9% local authorities and 62.8% private. The two biggest airports, Heathrow and Gatwick are privately owned. The most important 100% Council owned airport is Luton. Air traffic control is 51% private, 49% public with UKCG having a golden share of the latter.

No final decision has been taken on airport runways additions. Although the present Government are backing the third runway at Heathrow, the case for it is poor set against other more pressing concerns such as climate change, and the disruption its development would cause to the M25 and 10,000 households needing to be re-housed. The argument that aviation fuel is about to become sustainable aviation fuel (SAF) is not valid. SAF production is less than 1% of all fuel used and, although airlines would welcome it as no change to the aircraft is required to use it, it is far too expensive. That would only change if the UK and Europe (at minimum) would make it mandatory, so production volume could increase, and the cost come down. Regional airports to support business beyond London are not used sufficiently and could have growth potential for regional business.

Stanstead and London City airport expansions have been agreed, but the Gatwick second runway is still subject to further delay until debates about noise and access for public transport are resolved. In any case, the disruption at Gatwick would be minor compared to the colossal disruption proposed at Heathrow.

All UK roads are in UKCG or LA control except for the M6 toll road, which is privately owned. There are about 40,000 (unadopted) minor roads, owned by the residents.

SOLUTIONS
TRAINS
1   Re-privatise the rail network
Go back to privatising the network but the contractor would be responsible for railway maintenance as well as trains within its rail track area. Electrify diesel trains as soon as possible to support reducing impact on the climate.

2   Prioritise central signalling
Central signalling and maintenance involving multi-ownership track should be managed by UKCG in the same way as air traffic control, with UKCG having 49% shareholding, a golden share and 51% private ownership.

PLANES
1   Develop regional airports
Opening up regional airport runways to international traffic would greatly increase growth, particularly because the airport can act as an attractive hub for local business development particularly outside London. PSP, one of Canada's major pension fund investors have just acquired, through their subsidiary AviAlliance, our regional airports of Aberdeen, Glasgow and Southampton. AviAlliance have the facility to increase continental destinations for these airports. This follows another investment by US private equity fund Carlyle's acquisition of Southend airport in 2024.

2   Auction parking slots
In order to attract private funding for airport expansion in the regions, plane parking slots at airports could be auctioned on a high-level occupancy quota basis rather than a permanent docking allocation.

3   Cancel third runway at Heathrow

Cancel proposed investment in the third runway at Heathrow which would be highly disruptive to households and the M25 for a very long time, adversely affecting growth. Far better will be the proposed second runway at Gatwick, since the disruption is projected to be minimal to local infrastructure. Both decisions would help growth now.

ROADS

I   More toll roads

Greatly increase private construction of motorway or A road toll roads, particularly cross-country routes in England.

2   Improve road surfacing

A new specification for road surfacing is needed to reduce the possibility of potholes occurring, particularly important to reduce adverse impact on electric cars. Future road resurfacing should include this specification to avoid the built-in obsolescence which can occur. This may cost more in the short term, but the benefits long-term would be significant.

3   Increase the pothole budget

A budget of £3 billion a year is necessary to maintain roads: that increased expenditure will definitely aid growth and reduce time and money lost in vehicle repair.

4   More cycle lanes

Clearly marked and constructed cycle routes and lanes should be created wherever there is a serious road accident history.

CHAPTER II

Climate change
and the environment

Control	Should UKCG control this?	**YES**
Manage	Should UKCG manage this?	**YES**

This is an issue that affects the lives of everyone. UKCG policy control for the future protection of the population against global overheating and the management of that policy is crucial to ensure safeguarding targets are met. There are three critical areas worth consideration; air pollution, water contamination and waste disposal, particularly non-biodegradable items such as the many plastics and derivatives.

THE PROBLEMS

Climate change has the potential to change life and/or reduce life on planet Earth, consequently action taken by UKCG will not guarantee safety on its own. All other major governments need to act in the same way. The biggest polluters, USA and China, were recently taking climate change seriously until the arrival of President Trump but were probably not willing to say so for the economic reasons of maximising sales and use of their fossil fuels prior to the transition to renewables. China, for example is the world's leading developer of battery technology. The attitude of the US administration under President Trump at present is focused on continuing use of fossil fuels, mainly because the cost of doing so is lower in the USA than anywhere else, which fuels US exports and US domestic demand.

The recent imposition by the US of tariffs on imported goods is, however, likely to create domestic inflation which may well trigger a rethink on fossil fuels. On cars for example, the rapid increase in sales of Chinese electric vehicles and the inevitable concern of Tesla in the US could drive a rethink.

UKCG itself can only be expected to protect the public properly from the weather-related disasters we know about at the moment: extreme wind speed, flooding and wildfires, for example, because the effect of those on the population are clear. But we don't know what worse there may be to come, if net zero targets are ignored. The increasing environmental cost of public protection from weather damage in the future will probably require extra taxation, and UKCG needs to forewarn the public of this to explain its actions now.

RECOMMENDATIONS (IN THE ABSENCE OF A GLOBALLY AGREED SOLUTION)

- All potential construction of industrial buildings and domestic housing on areas of potential flooding should cease
- Existing housing areas flooded recently should be defined by the UKCG as capable of regeneration, or not capable. If not capable, people affected should be rehoused at UKCG expense as budgets allow.
- Water storage is likely to become increasingly important in Southern England and an increased number of reservoirs, and availability of water hydrants to resist hot summer fires, should be planned for now.
- Much higher winds of 100 miles an hour or more will destroy weak trees, temporary buildings and lightweight installations and signage. UKCG should issue a general statement to the population as to what to do to mitigate the effects of high winds.

- Reducing river pollution from toxic waste requires far greater priority than given at present, with substantial fines being increased for the known polluters. Equal pressure should be placed on large scale farmers and industries which are the biggest polluters.
- RefreshingUK (Chapter 1) could employ people to tidy and smarten up those parts of the country that need it, particularly removal of litter and monitoring waste disposal.
- UKCG grant support for homes to become 100% reliable on renewable sources of energy will eventually become essential. Investment in researching whether individual properties could be designed to have a combination of solar panels and wind turbine generators to be self-sufficient in electricity would clearly help avoid unsightly pylons.
- Encouraging the planting and care of trees would help soak up carbon dioxide from the polluted atmosphere, create shade for the hotter summers forecasted and help reduce the risk of flooding, especially in cities.
- It would help waste disposal efficiency if all Local Authorities adopted the same bin colour coding for segregating types of waste.
- Whilst the main way to reduce air pollution, which is greatest in big cities, is to reduce carbon emission by using only electric vehicles, UKCG should renew the ban on log fire heaters originally envisaged in 2022.
- I would leave farmers alone, unless they are the source of pollution, as they are following the country code of maintaining crop yields, improving biodiversity and protecting woodland, which I see no point in fundamentally changing.
- UKCG could encourage the public to seek to repair domestic items rather than replace them by running TV and social media

campaigns. There is a gradual movement towards repair as a way of reducing household costs, but repair of computers, electrical and electronic items is hard to find. The UKCG campaign would help restrain the increasing number of landfill sites, and also encourage the growth of repair businesses.

- UKCG should invest in biomass research to utilise waste produced by industrial and agricultural activity and promote methods of increasing biomass as a renewable source of energy, where it is cost effective to do so.

- UKCG should point out to its population the damaging effect that climate change could have on everyone's most precious possession, their home. This would help gain citizen support for what are otherwise viewed as unnecessary tax increases as and when UKCG will inevitably need to impose them in the future.

CHAPTER 12

Governing standards, fairness and censorship

Control	Should UKCG control this?	**YES**
Manage	Should UKCG manage this?	**YES**

THE PROBLEM

This book is ultimately about supporting the citizens of the UK. The context of this support is the growth agenda of UKCG and, by inference, growth is the ambition of all countries in the world in practice. I have said national growth can only occur if we as citizens get behind it. If we don't trust UKCG to always act in our reasonable interests, we won't feel comfortable and will do what we want, rather than align ourselves with what UKCG wants. If however the public start to feel that we are genuinely being heard and supported as a policy prerogative, we will both respond well and perhaps more importantly still, feel proud that we belong to a country that does so.

Today almost everyone uses some form of social media online. This has many positive advantages, particularly in obtaining information quickly. It also has a big disadvantage in that it allows rapid dissemination of false information and is often doing so. Social media is international: a benefit is that we can learn that other people are broadly no different to ourselves, a downside being that others can easily introduce us to things that are harmful, untrue or unhelpful. The younger you are, the greater this latter potential, because you will have less experience from which to judge the value of online content (one reason why voters should be at least 18 years old, in my view).

The lack of trust in politicians which developed particularly during the last Government, but has persisted with the present one, seriously damages growth in two ways. Firstly, people will tend to save rather than spend because they are not sure they can believe what they are being told about Government policy and intentions, particularly when the policy is growth, and UKCG's actions appear to be irrelevant to that objective: or that climate change is the number one priority, and then a third runway at Heathrow is supported and planning legislation does away with environmental protections. Or no more tax increases are planned in 2025, but the fiscal rules are broken, and they are the priority, so there may be more tax increases. Such contradictions have the effect of undermining belief in the value of government statements.

And secondly, the inability/unwillingness of UKCG to settle cases involving severe damage caused to citizens; for example, for those working in their roles within the Post Office, those given contaminated blood, and even the delay over financial compensation for the unfortunate man wrongly imprisoned for 17 years for a crime he did not commit, is making people wonder whether citizens are really valued. What does being 'British' mean? Why should I work hard if UKCG show no empathy for me when life gets tough? This is clearly antithetical to growth and damaging to any sense of belonging, especially if the underlying theme of the zeitgeist is becoming; *"We are all in trouble, the system is broken and it might get worse"*.

As the world's first democratic government by parliament of the people rather by dynastic rule, the historic culture of UK citizens is imbued with a sense of fairness and consideration for others. However recently UK citizens have progressively become concerned about abuse of power by UKCG politicians, and have developed a sense that there is one rule for UKCG, and a less favourable rule for ordinary citizens. There is now far less trust that UKCG government politicians will genuinely put the interests of the UK citizens before the interests of themselves. Under our voting system, which rewards a single mindset on running the country rather than a consensus of views, there is a marked tendency for those members of the party in power to become somewhat arrogant and insensitive, or to act in ways that suggest this. This is a potentially serious problem that, if not overcome, could result in a breakdown of civil order.

Regarding censorship, it is not clear if freedom of speech allows anything to be said or written and what, if anything must to be censored by UKCG. There is no obvious public mandate for any form of censorship. The law of blasphemy was abolished in 2008. The UK law on libel places the burden of proof of innocence on the defendant. That would seem unreasonable, since it tacitly invites anyone to attempt to defame another person's character without evidence. Incitement to harm the public is a mandate to apply censorship by law. Article 20 of the United Nations International Convention on Human Rights forbids incitement to harm (ICCPR).

There have been various attempts by the previous government to repeal or modify the European Convention on Human Rights (ECHR). There are rumours that the Labour government would also like to change those rights.

RECOMMENDATION

The ECHR should not be changed since it remains relevant for UKCG citizens.

These rights are set out on the following pages: I believe they are of great benefit to UK citizens and should not be tampered with.

THE EUROPEAN CONVENTION ON HUMAN RIGHTS AND PROTOCOLS TO THE CONVENTION (ECHR) *(simplified version)*

NOTE *This simplified version was prepared by the Directorate of Communication of the Council of Europe for educational purposes only. The only texts which have a legal basis are to be found in the official published versions of the Convention for the Protection of Human Rights and Fundamental Freedoms and its protocols.*

Article 1	**Obligation to respect human rights** *States must ensure that everyone has the rights stated in this Convention.*
Article 2	**Right to life** *You have the right to life.*
Article 3	**Prohibition of torture** *No one ever has the right to hurt you or torture you. Even in detention your human dignity has to be respected.*
Article 4	**Prohibition of slavery and forced labour** *It is prohibited to treat you as a slave or to impose forced labour on you.*
Article 5	**Right to liberty and security** *You have the right to liberty. If you are arrested you have the right to know why. If you are arrested you have the right to stand trial soon, or to be released until the trial takes place.*
Article 6	**Right to a fair trial** *You have the right to a fair trial before an unbiased and independent judge. If you are accused of having committed a crime, you are innocent until proved guilty. You have the right to be assisted by a lawyer who has to be paid by the state if you are poor.*

Article 7 **No punishment without law**
You cannot be held guilty of a crime if there was no law against it when you did it.

Article 8 **Right to respect for private and family life**
You have the right to respect for your private and family life, your home and correspondence.

Article 9 **Freedom of thought, conscience and religion**
You have the right to freedom of thought, conscience and religion. You have the right to practise your religion at home and in public and to change your religion if you want.

Article 10 **Freedom of expression**
You have the right to responsibly say and write what you think and to give and receive information from others. This includes freedom of the press.

Article 11 **Freedom of assembly and association**
You have the right to take part in peaceful meetings and to set up or join associations including trade unions.

Article 12 **Right to marry**
You have the right to marry and to have a family.

Article 13 **Right to an effective remedy**
If your rights are violated, you can complain about this officially to the courts or other public bodies.

Article 14 **Prohibition of discrimination**
You have these rights regardless of your skin colour, sex, language, political or religious beliefs, or origins.

Article 15   Derogation in time of emergency

In time of war or other public emergency, a government may do things which go against your rights, but only when strictly necessary. Even then, governments are not allowed, for example, to torture you or to kill you arbitrarily.

Article 16   Restrictions on political activity of aliens

Governments may restrict the political activity of foreigners, even if this would be in conflict with Articles 10, 11 or 14.

Article 17   Prohibition of abuse of rights

Nothing in this Convention can be used to damage the rights and freedoms in the Convention.

Article 18   Limitation on use of restrictions of rights

Most of the rights in this Convention can be restricted by a general law which is applied to everyone. Such restrictions are only allowed if they are strictly necessary.

Articles 19 to 51

These articles explain how the European Court of Human Rights works.

Article 34   Individual applications

If your rights contained in the Convention have been violated in one of the member states you should first appeal to all competent national authorities. If that does not work out for you, then you may appeal directly to the European Court of Human Rights in Strasbourg.

Article 52   Inquiries by the Secretary General

If the Secretary General of the Council of Europe requests it, a government must explain how its national law protects the rights of this Convention.

PROTOCOLS TO THE CONVENTION

Article 1 of Protocol No. 1   Protection of property
You have the right to own property and use your possessions.

Article 2 of Protocol No. 1   Right to education
You have the right to go to school.

Article 3 of Protocol No. 1   Right to free elections
You have the right to elect the government of your country by secret vote.

Article 2 of Protocol No. 4   Freedom of movement
If you are lawfully within a country, you have the right to go where you want and to live where you want within it.

Article 1 of Protocol No. 6   Abolition of the death penalty
You cannot be condemned to death or executed by the state.

Article 2 of Protocol No. 7   Right of appeal in criminal matters
You may appeal to a higher court if you have been convicted for committing a crime.

Article 3 of Protocol No. 7   Compensation for wrongful conviction
You have the right to compensation if you have been convicted for committing a crime and it turns out that you were innocent.

Article 1 of Protocol No. 12   General prohibition of discrimination
You cannot be discriminated against by public authorities for reasons of, for example, your skin colour, sex, language, political or religious beliefs, or origins.

RECOMMENDATIONS ON STANDARDS AND FAIRNESS

1 End favoritism in UKCG appointments

Obviously the objective of UKCG should be to regain public trust in the fairness of the behaviour of UKCG policy controllers and other employees. The first urgent act is for UKCG personnel to refrain from appointing policy makers and policy advisers purely on the basis of financial donations, group lobbying or close friendship, and appoint such people on merit and relevance alone.

2 Act promptly on misconduct

UKCG employees are human and entitled to be fallible on occasions. When their behaviour is discovered to be potentially against civil or criminal law the person concerned should be suspended immediately from office pending a resolution of the issue. Too frequently in the past, UKCG employees, often supported by senior UKCG managers, have been allowed to remain in post during an investigatory period. The effect of that is to undermine public trust in Government.

3 Create a UKCG Advice Ombudsman

Invite more easy access for UK citizens to provide constructive support and criticism directly to UKCG personnel. At present communication is entirely UKCG to citizens and there is no formal citizens to UKCG route. 100,000 signatures necessary for a parliamentary debate is the nearest we come to this.

In Denmark, for example, there is an ombudsman appointed by parliament for the sole purpose of ensuring citizens are fairly treated by the state.* That country welcomes input from other countries in achieving that purpose too, and UKCG should look seriously at

* en.ombudsmanden.dk

adopting that concept. That would send a powerful message to UK citizens that UKCG seriously cares about and wants to be trusted by UK citizens.

4   Allow funding of group actions

When UKCG is shown to have acted illegally, the law should allow citizens to group together to require UKCG to arrange reparation or sue UKCG in the event of UKCG intransigence (*see* Chapter 4). The Post Office and Infected Bloods scandals already mentioned are examples of why imperilled citizens cannot at present trust UKCG. This recommendation also affects growth psychologically (*see* Chapter 1).

5   Admit failure as well as success

UKCG Ministers should learn that it is OK to admit failures with an explanation as to why the event happened and why it went wrong, and evidence action has been taken to ensure it will not happen again. This does not happen, because Ministers assume that the public will think they are incompetent. In reality, the public is more likely to forgive and forget and have trust in the human with the courage to admit failure.

Also, if a Minister has clearly erred, the public will retain and remember this information until the Minister admits it, leaving the public without trust in that Minister or those supporting them for longer than is helpful to UKCG. This provision also applies to UKCG employees withholding relevant information helpful to defendants in a UK Court of Law.

6   Treat citizens equally

UKCG should treat citizens fairly and avoid one rule for one, and a different rule for others. Currently, the most egregious examples of this are the difference in pension funding for UKCG employees (no ring-fenced fund to meet future pension liabilities) and private sector employees (separate ring-fenced funds required by law to meet future liabilities) (*addressed in* Chapter 1), and the regulatory enforcement for private companies to have their accounts audited: but no such regulatory enforcement for the 153 Local Government Authorities.

RECOMMENDATIONS ON CENSORSHIP

All the issues covered by this chapter fundamentally affect the ability and interest of citizens and groups of citizens to make progress through trust, mutual understanding, have discussions that focus on a reasonable outcome that are not derailed by exchange of personal insults and have contact through channels that are not biased or distorted. Only once such changes are made will citizens feel safe and comfortable enough to pursue a growth agenda. Those with the power to create radical change must also explain why, and invite opinion before action, as it will be rare indeed if those in positions of power have got it exactly right first time! This psychological preparedness for growth is, I feel, ultimately the most important condition which will determine whether growth actually occurs or not.

What speech, written or oral, should be censored? The origin of censorship concerns people becoming upset about personal insult, personal faith or personal political views. All of these will happen whether they are censored or not, so the issue is whether anyone or any organisation should be punished for saying something and, if so, what the nature of that punishment should be.

There is no UKCG mandate for acting on any of these issues, but I am proposing that UKCG nevertheless has a moral obligation to manage them as being in the interests of citizens and UKCG in equal measure.

On matters of religion, the UKCG is not secular, whereas most of the world's governments are. The UK, to the extent that 'Lords Spiritual' who comprise a part of the unelected House of Lords can have an effect on the laws of the UK, is not a secular state.

Many secular states happily recognise the historical association of religious belief within state institutions such as schools, the UK included. When it comes to censorship, it can be assumed that a secular state would be more tolerant of the roles, rules and history of religious belief but not to the extent of politicising that belief in policy. For the UK that view is slightly harder to maintain whilst the Church of England has a potential power of legal veto on policy.

I recommend that the Lords Spiritual should be abandoned as a part of the House of Lords to make it easier for UKCG to pronounce on free speech. That would also make the UK a secular state like most others. I have faith that this would have popular support.

When it comes to censorship of any sort, it is important to make a distinction between faith and belief in terms of motives and actions. In the public realm, *faith* is having a sense that someone is capable of doing something, whereas *belief* is the thought that someone will actually do something. For example, *"My wife would be good as a babysitter"* (faith) or *"It will be fine when my wife babysits"* (belief). In other words, belief implies action to prove faith, whereas faith alone does not. Belief can therefore impinge on other person's rights and could be censored, but not faith.

In censorship too it is important to distinguish between truth and validity. Truth is a question of fact which can be evidenced: validity is a logical argument which defines a probability of truth.

"I was waiting outside when Fred stole the radio from the shop" could be censored (because it was known Fred was not the thief) whereas, *"I only saw one man going into the shop who I recognised as Fred and I saw him leave with a bag under his arm at the time the*

theft was reported" is a valid argument which should not be censored but is not necessarily true (the thief was proven to be someone already in the shop before and after Fred came in and out, verified from the radio serial number which was not Fred's radio serial number recorded in the sales at the shop).

In other words, censoring valid argument or an invalid statement, however dangerous, is not legally possible until the truth is finally known. Anything else could be fake news. That is the limitation of censorship. That effectively leaves only one avenue for censorship which is incitement to harm, including personal abuse or to break the law. These are now already covered by UKCG in the Online Safety Act 2023 and the Equality Act 2010.

As I stated at the beginning of this chapter, social media is an important part of social interaction and has its benefits and disadvantages. Enforcement of the limitations of freedom of speech under the Online Safety Act against website owners can ultimately only be in the form of a UKCG threat to take down the site until the abusive content is removed.

We are all both public and private people. We are in this together, on one planet. We should focus on what we can agree, not on what we disagree about, and respect that we can be wrong and acknowledge that too. People can have different views to our own but if some of those views obviously and deliberately incite harm for UK citizens, they must be censored and UKCG must demand offending websites be closed down.

CHAPTER 13

A balance sheet to date

There is an underlying theme in all the financial solutions and proposals I have offered, and that is to build up UK citizens' interest in and willingness to support a growth agenda, on the basis that they see UKCG taking action to prove it really believes in the value of growth for everyone.

In the table below, I have summarised in a very broad way the financial impact of my Part 1 recommendations. I accept that these figures represent a hugely subjective account, and its only merit is to provide a basis for argument and to show that I appreciate that any policy may have unforeseen consequences.

I fundamentally believe that creating conditions for a fairer, safer and more inclusive society for citizens, with more trust in UKCG and thus a greater willingness to work more productively, a shared focus on growth in personal and trading terms and a liberal sense of humour will gives us an average of at least 2% growth for the next four years, meaning our GDP would increase to £2.81 trillion by year end April 2029 (using an estimate of £2.6 trillion in year ending March 2025). This compares with 0.75% per annum currently foreseen by the Bank of England in the immediate future, which would mean a GDP in four years of £2.68 trillion.

I have divided this financial summary into two aspects. The first is to assume that the October 2024 budget tax changes had been replaced by my budget, and the second is to take the spending increase for new capital projects in the budget, which suggested £20 billion a year for five years, and compare that to my proposed spending increases in Chapters 1 to 12 for the first year 2025/26.

The changes to inheritance tax in the October 2024 Budget are not happening in May 2025, so they are ignored. They will, however, have an effect from 2027, which I believe will have an adverse impact on growth at and possibly before that change.

Overall, the tax changes in the October Budget, excluding capital gains tax changes which I would accept, was a tax increase of £24 billion on business national insurance and an estimated loss of £4 billion resulting from the exodus of non-doms, a net increase of £20 billion. The motive for the size of this tax increase was stated to be the 'black hole' of £22 billion left by the previous government. As the OBR has since confirmed this could only be £9.5 billion, I have used the same logic and made my net tax rises conservatively at £10.4 billion as follows:

TAX PROPOSAL	£BILLION
Increasing business NI to 14% instead of 15%	3
10% increase in VAT	17
Initial cost of corporation tax reduction	-7
Cost of supporting carers' income tax relief	-1.2
New tax rate over £100,000 annual pay	-1.4
TOTAL TAX INCREASE	**10.4**

Predicting the effect of both approaches beyond the first year takes us into fantasy land so I can only highlight the most obvious spending cut I would propose, which is a reduction in the number of civil servants and quangos, which I have estimated at £7 billion before redundancy costs. At this early stage of searching for growth, I would not touch the welfare bill other than to root out fraud which I suspect is huge. I think it is bad policy to hurt the citizens most in need of support when you are trying to get them onside in pursuit of growth, let alone, as I stated earlier, inhumane.

Lowering costs through reducing the size of the civil service

If I assume that 100,000 civil servants (roughly the number recruited for Brexit) were made redundant, the annual saving would be £4.5 billion, using the average official cost of a civil servant as £45,000, excluding the one-off cost of redundancy. I have also questioned the validity and worth of countless quangos having an influence over policy and would aim to remove most of those and replace them with specific one-off policy implementation taskforces as and when needed by UKCG. I assume that an overall saving of £7 billion would be made. If all of the staff made redundant retrained, there would be a tax cost of £0.8 billion under my proposal to allow up to £4,000 of retraining expenses to be deducted from their gross income for up to four years after redundancy before it is assessed for income tax.

The reaction so far (February 2025) to the Budget measures has been that food prices are expected to rise by 5%, which is badly affecting the poorest sections of the population and is the result of the imposition of higher national insurance charges for business from April 2025. In contrast, the inflation cost of VAT increasing by 10% would be a 1% increase in vatable products and services. Hiring staff has almost ceased. I doubt if the tariff war instigated by the USA primarily aimed at China will harm my growth strategy, since it will simply encourage us to act in our own growth interests more quickly. In any case, the inflationary effect on USA citizens is likely to force an end to the tariff strategy quite soon.

My best estimate would be 1.5% growth for 2025/26 and at

least 2% each year after. If the current policies are not changed, I think growth will be negative (2025/26) and we will quickly enter recession.

In the October 2024 Budget UKCG did propose a capital expenditure of £20 billion for one year. By my reckoning, £15 billion of that would need to go on defence.

PART 2
Broad changes for the future

Voting and democracy

In the Introduction to this book I set out some assumptions about human behaviour and pointed out that only 20% of the population entitled to vote voted for the present Government, and 40% did not vote at all. I also suggested that people did not appear to believe that voting would help them have a better life.

I believe we should change our voting system immediately to be by proportional representation (PR) rather than the first-past-the-post system practised in the UK, the USA, Canada and India, but not elsewhere in major democratic countries where PR is used.

The logic of this is quite simple. Politics should not be like a boxing ring with someone in the red corner versus someone in the blue corner. People are multicoloured politically in their views on what is important to them and for others, and do not deserve to be given a label of left or right wing. It is quite OK to have views that could be both. Everyone should have a voice when voting: that voice needs a candidate (a range from diverse backgrounds) and those candidates need to have a chance of winning a seat in Parliament. Were that the case, I believe it would bring a greater feeling of togetherness and tolerance in politics and a sense of worth in knowing we all belong to a tolerant country. I would hope anyone persuaded by this book will add their name to the UK movement calling for a fresh freedom of voting expression - PR!

If we take the last UK general election results and look at them using the present system and then using proportional representation (purely in the sense of the number of the individual votes cast), then the result is a 'hung parliament', meaning no one party had a large enough majority to make policy changes alone. This is in fact therefore the truest view from the electorate as to what should happen from voting; which is, a consensus of views must be found when making policy.

The PR system is normally based on the single transferable vote system (STV), a system in which a voter in an area with a number of seats available places a number against all the names on the ballot paper. If there are six candidates, the voter puts each one in order of preference, with number one being the most desired and a compulsory vote and number six being the least desired. The winner has to reach the quota of votes set by the number of seats available for an area. To reach that quota will require eliminating some other candidates and transferring voter second preferences to remaining candidates and so on until a winner emerges.

For example, instead of the UK having 650 voting areas each voting for one MP as now, we would have 130 voting areas, each selecting five MPs, and let's say with ten candidates to put in order of preference as in the example above. The winner has to reach the quota of votes set by the number of seats available for an area. Thereafter the Number two votes are counted, and so on, until five MPs emerge. With the UK voting population being around 48 million, each of the 130 areas would consist of around 370,000 voters and there would be five MPs electable for that area, so one MP for 74,000 voters. A great chance for a variety of views!*

This is the difference between the actual party split of the 650 MPs from the 2024 UK general election and a theoretical PR

---

* An example of how this system works can be found at electoral-reform. org.uk/voting-systems/types-of-voting-system/single-transferable-vote/

party split based on the proportion of national vote.

	Actual	Under PR
Labour	411	219
Conservative	121	154
Reform	5	93
Liberal Democrats	72	79
Green	4	44
Scotland, Wales, NI + Independent	37	61
Total Seats	650	650
Total votes cast	28.8 million	28.8 million
% of eligible voters	59.7	59.7

A PR result would be different to that shown due to the way STV works, but the principle is clear enough.

THE FIRST-PAST-THE-POST SYSTEM: A NUMBER OF DRAWBACKS

Firstly, each political party has a pre-set position on several key policy issues. This will take precedence over the interests of all citizens in a number of ways:

a) Candidates selected by political parties will be those whose views clearly reflect the pre-selected ones of the party concerned.

b) When candidates become MPs, they are pressurised to vote for their party even when their conscience dictates they should not. A recent example of this was the concern of some Labour party MPs about the withdrawal of the winter fuel allowance for many pensioners.

c) Many people will feel that there is no point in voting in areas where traditionally there has been an overwhelming majority for one party. In my area in the local council elections, for example, the Liberal Party candidate stated that there was no point in voting Labour because the area has always been a Conservative or Liberal candidate: forgetting perhaps that the Liberal Party is the only one in favour of proportional representation!

d) Our first-past-the-post system allows a party to be autocratic and take urgent and decisive action, whether desirable or not, in an emergency, such as military invasion, civil disturbance or a pandemic. Whilst this will also happen in a government formed by proportional representation it might take a little longer to gain consensus as to what needs to be done. However that longer process might prevent overtly draconian measures to take root as occurred when Boris Johnson attempted to prorogue parliament in 2019.

Autocratic government may be superficially attractive to frustrated activists, but those activists will normally be a minority of the whole population. Our system of voting encourages the opposition at election time to rubbish and distort the efforts of the incumbent government under the slogan *"We need change"*, often with no clear policy alternative mentioned, and that can incite violence as well as peaceful protest.

Secondly, there is an inevitability that a so-called left wing or right wing government will create policies to cancel out each other's previous policies, which occurs simply because there is no real consensus on policy from the public, only a desire for 'change'. But 'change' does not mean anything, neither modification nor cancellation of previous policy; just a 'blank canvas' for the incoming administration.

The insistence of the present UKCG that the previous government left a mess is a typical example, as is President Trump's repudiation of many Jo Biden policies in the USA without defining the consequences for the public. In the UK, this vagueness leaves citizens in a void, not knowing what anyone stands for and wondering what will come next. Those on the left worry about what a right-wing government will do to them, and vice versa. This does nothing for a sense of belonging, as citizens remain unsure of what sort of UK they belong to.

The language of politicians who frequently apply hyperbole to their own performance without taking the effect on the population into account is also a feature which irritates the public. In June 2024, the National Centre for Social Research reported that a record 45% of the public 'almost never' trust governments of any party to place the needs of the nation above their own party.*

Thirdly, a first-past-the-post government has greater potential to apply inappropriate pressure on established institutions to accept government interference, such as withholding information in a civil or criminal court case on the grounds of a breach of national security, or be unwilling to provide particularly compromising information under the freedom of information laws. That would still be possible, but less likely under proportional representation.

Finally, and most important of all, first-past-the-post government quickly divides the population into more extreme and somewhat simplistic factions, particularly if conditions are tough. The rise of Reform in the UK is an example of this, as is the current tension in the USA between Democrat and Republican. The result damages what should be pride in country and faith in its people and in Government. Such divisions are also bad for growth and bad for relationships

* Trust and confidence in Britain's system of government at record low: National Centre for Social Research

between citizens. The benefits of proportional representation are similar in scope to what can occur in the UK parliament when there is a free vote according to conscience.

The turnout of 59.7% was the lowest (excluding the 2001 turnout of 59.6%) for 100 years. Perhaps this is a hint of dissatisfaction with the system? According to YouGov polling, twice as many people say they would prefer PR to the current first-past-the-post system and have done so consistently for many years.

The Liberal party is the only political party in the UK which espouses proportional representation and that could well mean they have less power than they have now (although the table above might suggest otherwise were PR to be introduced). You will know from reading the scene-setting Introduction of this book that I strongly favour the adoption of PR as our electoral voting system as a matter of urgency, so that the mix of opinions within Parliament can properly reflect the strength of support for them in the country.

When it comes to growth, public consensus becomes crucial. When it comes to big decisions on climate change, tax, defence and protection under the law, PR is essential.

CHAPTER 15

Long term debt and the emotions behind it

Debt is not just a numbers game: it is an investment for somebody. And, like all investments, it is a gamble as much based on emotional 'feel' as known facts. The feelings come from being hopeful, but actually not knowing what will happen tomorrow. As much as growth flourishes in the right atmosphere, so does a willingness to lend to UKCG and for UKCG to be able to borrow.

A lot has been written about this, and argument seems to fall into two camps: firstly, there will be a day of reckoning and secondly, there won't be a day of reckoning. Who is likely to be right? Since UKCG policy is to try not to increase debt further, and it is not succeeding, should it bother?

The answer can partly be found by looking at other countries. If we look at Japan, the USA and the UK we can compare these debt percentages to GDP, as at the end of 2023 according to the IMF:

Japan	249.67%
USA	123.01%
UK	101.15%

So why are we so concerned, when Japan appears not to be? The answer is that debt is only one side of the balance sheet. The other side is government financial assets. In Japan, in 2023, for example, the government had a social security fund, which was 55% of GDP in value, as well as other financial assets, which brought the level of net debt down to around 120% of GDP. In the UK, however, the financial assets are very small so that net debt is almost the same as debt itself. That is also true in principle for the USA, which is why both countries should be concerned about debt increasing each year. So, if the borrower is concerned, so might the lender be. This is where emotions take over from numbers.

AVOIDING APOCALYPSE NOW

The International Monetary Fund (IMF) estimated world debt at 237% of global GDP in 2023. Why do people keep lending to governments? The answer is that the underlying assets to cover payment are ultimately held in the hands of the citizens, not the governments. In the UK for example, net worth (assets less liabilities) in 2023 was £12.2 trillion, of which £11 trillion was household net worth according to the ONS (Office for National Statistics). I would suggest therefore that lenders to the UKCG would rely on UKCG taxing the wealth of UK households as security for their loans and the same would apply in the USA, where household wealth is greater than State wealth.

So, can we carry on borrowing? Yes, if we do not mind taxing the wealth of households through capital taxes to pay the debt interest: but that constrains future generations in every way, because increasingly, all taxes will do is pay the interest on debt, already at 10% of government spending today. It could also encourage wealthy taxpayers in the UK to emigrate.

But the huge new factor today however, is the impact of climate change on household assets, particularly housing. Huge fires in Los Angeles, flooding in the UK, Spain, Polynesia, the Caribbean and Asia, and multiple cases of higher winds, drought and extreme rainfall have already depleted household assets throughout the world.

The crudest and biggest single reason for fighting climate change is to avoid the erosion of citizen's financial assets which are now the basis of lending to Governments. Not to fight to do so invites a collapse of world financial order.

In order to think about reducing UKCG debt levels, we need to consider the role of the Bank of England, the lender of last resort. Bank lending in general works on the principle that you lend to an illiquid institution or person if they are solvent, solvency meaning the borrower's financially assessed assets are seen to be greater than the money lent by a good margin. The size of lending risk is discounted by the rate of interest charged: the higher the risk, the higher the interest charged.

Bank lending has always been a tricky business as those who deal in house mortgages well know. Asset value can fall and solvency be questioned. Cash flow can be subject to wild fluctuations. Allowing a borrower time to recover may or may not be preferable to taking a loss now. The same thinking applies to UKCG lenders, including the Bank of England. UKCG have to ensure that the market perception is that a loan to them will be repaid from liquidity.

The Bank of England is supposed to control price inflation in the UK economy. In practice this is not possible as inflation is caused by matters beyond the Bank's control such as the price of oil, for example, or the war in Ukraine. In any case, inflation is not instant: it is a progressive dynamic pressure which takes time to appear and disappear. It would make more sense to me to ask the Bank to control something it can control, and that is the base interest rate. In my view it would be more stabilising to ask the Bank to control the base interest rate in a range of 3-4.5% and ensure policy reflects that. That would give markets more stability than a 2% inflation target which is likely to be regularly exceeded. One good reason why price inflation is here to stay above 2% is because it is the plus side of growth and greater added value. Inflation can also erode debt and may be the only way to reduce debt in the future in democratic countries. In banking, high inflation of asset prices has a positive effect on solvency.

Setting a mid-field base interest rate should also help more UK citizens, particularly the less well off. Violent fluctuations between zero% and 10% and beyond only benefit the rich, whereas the vast majority of citizens want a reliable financial environment so that they can plan their saving and spending with confidence that their mortgage or borrowing costs, for example, will remain as fixed as possible; and that will aid growth.

What level an interest rate is at also presents an investment challenge for UKCG and all businesses. Interest rates at 10% per annum means you have to get your financial return on capital investments very quickly (inside 10 years), whereas an interest rate of 3.5% per annum gives you a lot more time (inside 28 years) to get a financial return and is therefore a level far better for motivating UKCG and private sector industry to want to invest in major infrastructure projects for example, and therefore would be good for growth. Since most large UKCG investments have at best a capital return of 25 years at best, that makes investment decisions by UKCG somewhat limited at present.

Finally, the best UKCG can do to reduce debt is to continuously create the right atmosphere for growth. That will have the biggest emotional effect on lenders and help UKCG to keep debt interest low. In order to do this, there needs to be a change in mindset. Lending to start-up businesses without asset back-up, particularly to software start-ups, needs to increase. In the USA, banks have tended to take risks with start-ups such as Amazon in the 1990's well before profitability and asset backing was in sight. UK banks are more cautious, and lending to software start-ups tends to be by 'angel' investors (previously successful business people keen to help).

In a survey by the Sunday Times in January 2025 of the top 50 fastest growing UK 'tech' businesses, the businesses were divided into two equal types: 50 in software and 50 in hardware development. Only 16% of the top tech software businesses were outside London, whereas 64% of the hardware businesses were outside the capital. This suggests that banking attitudes to ideas-based business are London-centric, but attitudes to hardware are more widespread. It also reflects a certain risk reluctance to support software which of course is the engine of hardware.

If UKCG goes for growth in a big way, tax revenue will rise sharply and the government will be able to properly invest in public services. UKCG borrowings will reduce proportionately, and households will spend more as their assets will have risen. They will be able to borrow more against those assets, and they'll feel better as they see genuine improvement in their lives and environment.

THE TRADE DEFICIT AND THE EFFECT ON DEBT

The UK trade deficit - where the value of UK imports exceeds the value of UK exports - has long been a feature of our economy. As already stated, we currently have a net trading deficit with the rest of the world and that clearly affects the amount we have to borrow. We also trade in a currency which is not a major trading currency as are the Euro, US dollar or Chinese Yuan. That means the cost of our exports can change quickly to good or bad effect, and investors would naturally favour the most traded currencies in their choice of long-term affiliation. Overall, the balance of trade is not critical for growth providing the balance is not excessively negative (above 6% of GDP): far more important is encouraging home business growth which would naturally positively affect exports anyway.

FISCAL RULES

UK governments frequently invent fiscal rules such as total borrowings must not be greater than GDP, or capital expenditure must not be more than 3% of GDP. Currently the fiscal rule is that annual UK income should equal annual UK expenditure by 2029/30. This is not a rule of course, it is a hope, and a sensible one. It is often the case that the way the comparator is calculated is suddenly changed when it appears the rule will be broken, thus making the rule pointless in the first place. There is no point in having any rule unless there is a credible plan to go with it.

At present, there is no credible plan to meet the current fiscal rule. As a result, it is probable that total debt will increase. That is one of the reasons for writing this book - only growth, greater productivity or inflation or any combination of these will have a chance of meeting the present fiscal rule.

Fortunately, most UK citizens are smart, and are likely to have a net positive asset value - meaning their accumulated wealth is greater that any outstanding debt. They probably don't have any particular fiscal rules, apart perhaps from remembering what our grandmothers might have said: *"Don't spend beyond your means!"*.

CHAPTER 16

Relationship with other countries: a world view

As a general principle, working together is better than working apart. It's important to remember that the actions of foreign governments do not necessarily reflect the majority wishes and opinions of the people who live there. That can also apply to democracies!

It would be reasonable to assume that the people who run democracies which use the PR system of voting to appoint their leaders are more likely to have a population which agrees broadly with that government's actions. The more autocratic the government, the less likely it will be that the citizens of that country are of the same opinion as those who run their country. This statement is based on my people assumptions outlined in the Introduction to this book.

There are several fundamental reasons for UKCG to have good relationships with every country, irrespective of whether UKCG or its citizens approve of the actions of some nations.

> • We all live on and share the same planet, and thus are all affected by climate change
> • We all have to defend our populations from harm
> • We all have to trade with each other to live

The extent to which individual countries are willing or able to engage in cooperation with others is the underlying challenge for UKCG foreign relations. The fact remains however that we all rely on each other.

CLIMATE CHANGE

The biggest world issue at the moment concerns the three fundamentals listed above, of which the most important is climate change. This is simply because no or limited action presents a possibility of wiping out the population of our planet.

It might be worth considering what has driven human progress since human beings came into existence. The first humans were born in the hottest part of the Earth in Africa, the sun was the greatest influence on life and indeed worshipped. Gradually, humanity drifted north in search of easy access to water. It was water which provided better food and greater activity leading to over 4,000 years of warfare in the parts of the earth which could sustain and supply conquering armies.

Rapidly fast forwarding, it was Europeans who occupied the land of the indigenous peoples of Africa, Australasia, Asia and the Americas and up until the latter part of the nineteenth century, growth came from conquest in the form of empire in both East and West. From the beginning of the twentieth century until today, the climate benefits of sun and rain began to be subsumed by the age of oil. Oil became the driver of growth, supported by electricity. But burning fossil fuels changes the Earth's climate and the availability of sunshine, rain and wind is changing. For the first time, climate is no longer the engine of growth: in fact, it could be the enemy of growth.

The fact that other nations are not acting at all, or quickly enough, to combat global warming is not a reason to stop us aiming for so-called net zero carbon emissions. The most urgent investment decision needed to be made by UKCG is therefore ensuring that all forms of renewable energy which will have to be the basis of energy generation in the future have direct access to the National Grid. The National Grid is an energy delivery organisation, not an energy creator. Capital investment in the means of the delivery of renewable energy to its users is therefore the number one investment priority for UKCG.

DEFENCE

Geographically our closest neighbours are the Europeans. We had close ties with the European Union (EU) until Brexit on 31st January 2020. Nevertheless, we are also members of the North Atlantic Treaty Organisation (NATO). This organisation also includes the USA and Canada, whose involvement and support saved the European allied population from military defeat in two world wars in the twentieth century, although that military support for maintaining Europe's borders is currently being questioned by President Trump. The military strength of the USA is far greater than the whole of the rest of NATO members combined. When the USA demands greater investment in defence from other NATO members we, UKCG, as a member, should respond forthwith by meeting the target of 2.5% of GDP and budget for 4% going forward. We cannot assume that the USA will always fight our cause. In fact, the probability is that the USA will soon leave NATO once the Europeans have clubbed together financially to support their borders effectively with sufficient military hardware.

TRADE

The decision to abandon free trade and free people movement with the European Union has impacted our growth prospects badly. This is not surprising, as the principle of imperilling export sales relations with existing customers in favour of an apparent freedom to act independently in trading with other nations outside the EU was always going to be a huge risk, not least because the only other countries capable of replacing lost EU sales are the USA and China. The power imbalance between the UK and either USA or China is obvious.

It follows that UKCG should, as a matter of urgency, repair the trade relationship with the EU and seek a free trade deal as a major part of a 'growth' policy and be prepared to compromise on freedom of movement of citizens.

UKCG also has close relations with English-speaking countries throughout the world such as Canada (a member of NATO), Australia and New Zealand. The existence of the Commonwealth of Nations also had a trading significance for UKCG, which could also be an engine of growth.

OVERSEAS REPRESENTATION AND SUPPORT

UKCG has always had overseas embassies with the purpose of fostering good relations and helping UK citizens operating in a foreign land. The latter role has been criticised as inadequate when urgent situations occur, such as the UK citizen withdrawal from Afghanistan under the Taliban takeover. An overseas embassy can play an important role in helping develop UK trade overseas and a growth agenda should be instilled in the embassy staff to the extent of helping UK citizens with contacts and operational support. Each consulate should have a trade and investment manager with appropriate civil service seniority and salary with a brief to pursue growth for the UK.

I do not believe that UKCG should be providing overseas investment itself as a way of improving relations, since at present we cannot afford the cost when so much investment is needed at home.

CHAPTER 17

Developing community feeling

A strong sense of community and a willingness to help others in adversity has always existed amongst UK citizens. The public are consistantly generous in donating to charities and to people suffering from natural or unexpected personal and national disasters.

The second world war was the last occasion when the UK population was truly united in self-preservation from danger. During the recent COVID pandemic UK citizens also cooperated peacefully with UKCG to stay at home to support the NHS, although a significant minority were concerned about the lockdown effect on children's education, and a further minority objected that their freedom was being constrained.

Generally however, in peacetime, there has been a gradual erosion of relational contact and community development. Amongst other factors too numerous to explore here, I believe this is due in part to the mobile phone and social media culture which has had an effect on personal relationships, even to the extent of creating family tension about censorship of what can be viewed on social media. I have often thought that trend started when the pram was replaced by the buggy. Babies in prams could see and interact with their parent in the outside world, whereas in the buggy, the baby faces the outside world and cannot see the person whose job is to help them feel secure in their world.*

* suzannezeedyk.com/how-buggies-shape-babies-brains/

IMPACT OF COVID

The social impact of the COVID outbreak has been dramatic, particularly in the UK. Working from home became a new possibility, approved by governmental and private employers as a necessity during the recovery from the outbreak. Yet COVID has also exposed another problem that been under the surface in the UK for some time, and that is the relationship between education and job opportunity. Many young people today are not sure what they want to do as adults and even not sure in fact what there actually is to do, which of course is constantly evolving.

Although every young person will have at least one specific gift and/or skill for which there will be career roles, too many young people are not in education, employment or training at the moment. The UK has the National Careers Service* which contains a section called *Take a skills test* which asks the young person to complete a questionnaire and offers careers advice building on their responses, free of charge. My concern for young people is that they may not know what strengths they have in employment potential terms, so this is worth doing. Also, In the USA for example, there is a career online test which aims to match the individual's skills with a job opportunity** which could also uncover a skill that is wanted elsewhere or not covered by the UK checklist.

The King's Trust*** is particularly helpful for young people seeking work: the website even includes advice on starting a business. And as I am promoting a growth agenda in this book, I'm offering young budding entrepreneurs a free simple financial test to find out whether they are likely to make money from their ideas at robertbtyler.com.

   * nationalcareers.service.gov.uk
  ** careerexplorer.com/career-test/
*** kingstrust.org.uk/how-we-can-help/programmes

The importance of this exploration to uncover skills and aptitudes particularly applies in towns and areas which have traditionally relied on major manufacturing activity to exist and thrive. Young people seeking employment and wanting to stay in their area of upbringing may well say *"There are no jobs for me"*. Many of these towns are in the North of England, South Wales and specific areas in Northern Ireland based on shipbuilding alongside Scotish towns affected by the decline in oil drilling. I am sure talented young brains in these areas can learn to exploit new technologies like AI, new clean energy opportunities and traditional artisan skills to bring prosperity to their home areas too.

COMMUNITY LIVING

The pressure to build new homes is also an opportunity to build community feeling. I touched on this idea when introducing the RefreshingUK programme, but I think we can go a lot further in two respects.

Firstly, new housing estates should come with basic amenities for families. With a background of building well over a million new homes in five years, there will be housing estates in semi-rural areas and high-rise flats in more city-centred areas. Both developments should have some basic amenity additions as a standard practice. For example, an electric car charging point centre attached to a shop/café stocking essentials, clear dog walking and cycle paths leading to green spaces, provision of allotment space for those without gardens, a recreation centre for children and young people and a community hall controlled for renting out by the local council to and for the local people which includes a kitchen, outside garden space and car park.

Secondly, our high streets at present look sad, neglected and quite empty in many parts of the country. Planning laws on types of use allowed are probably restricting flexible usage of empty retail space.

Small specialist shops are closing due to high rent and rates costs and from online competition which doesn't incur such costs. Parking has become difficult and expensive.

Our shopping centres should be a larger version of our local community by providing shared retail occupation, a range of recreational and information sharing facilities (such as the Citizens' Advice Bureau, tourist information or therapeutic help), and as many trees as possible to create shade and help with flood risk, enhancing the general sense and experience of wellbeing. In addition, why not invest in enlarged pavement areas to encourage open air eating and drinking when the weather allows or space for outdoor heaters in the winter months. Parking in towns should be free for the benefit of the community (along with those at hospitals for patients and their families).

Retail space should be shared at large buildings (1,000 square feet plus) and in very large spaces (3,000 square feet plus) a mixture of service-based and retail product-based businesses could share space within the same building. Planning laws would need to be relaxed. All these shared spaces could be available on renewable short term leases covering the essential rent, electricity and water supply to the building. Parking should be free as it is in retail parks. That should help build up existing town communities and boost shop sales (growth).

Equally, green space could be shared amongst different popular sport and recreation activities on a council rental basis with appropriate safeguards on site quality maintenance.

In both the local housing and the high street changes, provision should be made for working from home or near-home type working. Even on large housing developments, it would be sensible for community convenience to have a rentable office unit building with a meeting area within the housing complex. Throughout all new developments trees and bushes should be liberally planted in public spaces, ideally maintained by residents along with Council assistance.

CREATING THE FUTURE TOGETHER

Whether we like it or not, we are all involved in creating a more enjoyable potentially 100 year life on planet Earth, and the more we share our own views of how to achieve this, the more we will get a common understanding of what works for us all. This book is all about building inspiration, stimulating thought and discussion - and above all, action!

We start by recognising everyone has a right to exist and has worth and talent. But everyone needs hope as well, and hope comes from progress: progress comes from working together to bring about a change that works for all and is backed by all. To achieve that change, we all have to believe in a democracy where our vote counts. Because the change we want is one that we will actually agree enables us to be happier in experiencing life. My thoughts are that we have to use the idea of growth as the hope for changing our world for the better.

More young entrepreneurs making a success of their ideas, more young people learning what their skills are and enjoying exploiting them, more respect for the way of life and needs of other citizens, more consensus and involvement on key political decisions which affect all of us.

And for older citizens, confidence they will be cared for: faith in a system that supports and rewards the efforts of the younger generation, respects that they inherit what we have rightly or wrongly constructed: and realises that trust in our dealings from now on must be merited.

This all starts by changing the voting system in the UK to reflect the range of views of all citizens. Maybe then we will get the Government we actually want that makes us proud to be UK citizens. I very much hope that as a result of reading this book, you will support the petition for PR in the UK.

Conclusion

Throughout *Turnaround UK* I have tried to place citizens' needs and desires at the centre of a growth plan for our country. Only citizens can create growth. I believe growth is the way to build a better life for everybody. We all want a 'better' life, but 'better' could mean a variety of things to a variety of people; it might mean a better standard of living, it could also mean a better standard of care or more job opportunities for your children, even a reduction in street crime in your neighbourhood. More money helps most people: but a greater sense that the UK Government can be trusted to value citizens and takes our needs, interests and views seriously is also needed, and a greater clarity from government as to how citizens benefit from growth, would help everyone and encourage participation in this endeavour.

I have, I hope, made it clear that the primary but not only purpose of a growth policy is to use the fruits of growth to assist those in greatest need of help and support, particularly children and the disadvantaged. When seeking productivity gains within government spending, I have made it clear that the poor and disadvantaged should not be penalised since that profoundly undermines the point of seeking growth.

A guiding principle behind the practical growth-based policies I recommend is to help reduce anxiety within all our lives. The threat of wars today, the consequences of climate change and the worry that increasing national and personal debt creates are a background to the current aggression and intolerance in political and human relations, typified by anonymous, polarised and often extremist and harmful comments on social media making us all anxious to some extent. Anxiety within families, often fuelled by an inability to keep up with the ever-rising cost of living and less than adequate public services, inevitably permeates into our children.

It doesn't need to be like this. I have focused on things we can do right now. Make Government more accountable, accessible and trustworthy: invest more in addressing climate change and reducing energy costs: spend on missile defence, not missile attack: encourage young entrepreneurs: invest in more community policing: avoid capital taxpayer expenditure based on long term projects which rely on many future governments to agree to and control: help anxious children in school: make housing more affordable: ensure all health care is more accessible quickly and tax consumption (more paid by the rich) not jobs (more lost by the poor).

Further, I have tried to foster a sense of wanting to belong to the UK through major new initiatives on housing both to rent and to buy, and in the process of building to focus on community need, not just roofs over our heads. The principle of RefreshingUK is part of that idea. This will gradually provide more secure bases for the population who need proper shelter and want to live in a better environment. That sense of belonging can only occur if citizens start to trust the judgment of people in government rather than suspecting they care for themselves or their party more than us: which is why I have proposed improving citizens' relationships with our governing bodies at national and local levels.

Finally, I have stressed the time is right for proportional representation (PR). This would surely put citizens' actual views and perspectives at the heart of government. My guess is it is in the interests of both the traditional governing parties, Labour and Conservative, to vote for this to counter the rise of the Reform party, and the remaining parties would certainly benefit from it as well. So let's do it!

As I said in the Introduction, these are my ideas, following the logic of the priorities I have outlined and drawing on my experience and research. Having a different view is a good thing, having diversity of interest and approach is a good thing, so whether you agree with my solutions or not, I hope this book has provided you with food for thought and motivation to action.

My plea in the title of this book was to trust and empower UK citizens to create growth. The people who govern us are there to protect our interests and we need to be able to trust them to do so. They now say we must have growth: but when they say that, the only way to show us they mean it, is to follow the logic of that strategy, create the right growth environment within all their policies and trust us as citizens to deliver.

That is all I want our Government to do. Leave the rest to us; it will be safe in our hands.